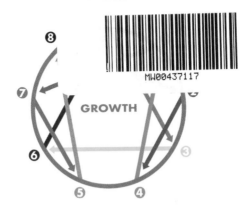

GROWTH

1 — SELF CONTROL · GOODNESS · TRUTH · PERFECTION · CLARITY · JUSTICE ·

2 — DISCERNING NEEDS · HELPFULNESS · ALTRUISM · LOVING · BOLD · SERVANTS HEART ·

3 — EXCELLENCE · EFFICIENCY · ACTION · ENCOURAGER · ESTABLISHER · INSPIRING ·

4 — EMOTIONALLY HONEST · CREATIVITY · EMPATHY · LOVE OF BEAUTY · SPACE SAVER ·

5 — HUMILITY · WISDOM · VISION · STEADFASTNESS · CLARITY · FAITHFULNESS ·

6 — FAITHFULNESS · COURAGE · GUARDIANSHIP · KINDNESS · LOYALTY · STRENGTH ·

7 — VISION · SPONTANEITY · JOY · THANKFULNESS · HOPE · LONG SUFFERING ·

8 — TENDERNESS · STRENGTH · ZEAL · VIGILANT · JUSTICE · PROTECTOR ·

9 — UNDERSTANDING · PEACE · KINDNESS · EMPATHY · PATIENCE · GENTLENESS ·

Elisabeth has a beautiful way of guiding the reader into a deeper understanding and self-awareness that leads to spiritual growth through the Enneagram. Through biblically sound and practical devotions, she helps you move from, "Okay, I know what type I am but what's next?" to personal, relational, and spiritual growth, so that you can live in the fullness of who you were created to be in your unique type.

—*Justin Boggs*
The Other Half Podcast
Enneagram coach, speaker, entrepreneur

If you know your Enneagram type and you're ready to make meaningful steps toward growth, this book is for you. Elisabeth combines her Enneagram expertise with her deep faith to guide readers toward self-understanding, growth, and transformation through contemplative yet practical writing. This devotional is a great tool that you'll return to again and again.

—*Steph Barron Hall*
Nine Types Co.

the
CHALLENGER

GROWING AS AN ENNEAGRAM

60-DAY
ENNEAGRAM DEVOTIONAL

the
CHALLENGER

GROWING AS AN ENNEAGRAM

ELISABETH BENNETT

WHITAKER
HOUSE

Introduction images created by Katherine Waddell.
Photo of Elisabeth Bennett by Jena Stagner of One Beautiful Life Photography.

THE CHALLENGER
Growing as an Enneagram 8

www.elisabethbennettenneagram.com
Instagram: @enneagram.life
Facebook.com/enneagramlife

ISBN: 978-1-64123-578-5
eBook ISBN: 978-1-64123-579-2
Printed in the United States of America
© 2021 by Elisabeth Bennett

Whitaker House
1030 Hunt Valley Circle
New Kensington, PA 15068
www.whitakerhouse.com

Library of Congress Control Number: 2021941179

1 2 3 4 5 6 7 8 9 10 11 ⨆⨆ 28 27 26 25 24 23 22 21

DEDICATION

To all the Eights holding this devotional,
you will never be betrayed by God.
You can hold fast to Him without fear.

Contents

FOREWORD

My therapist first introduced me to the Enneagram when I was in the trenches of an eating disorder during my sophomore year of high school. She pulled *The Enneagram Made Easy* by Elizabeth Wagele and Renee Baron from her bookshelf and handed it to me. I spent the week before my next appointment devouring each word on every page. Fascinated by the different types and wings, I suddenly had a new lens by which to see and understand the world and the people in my life—but also, most importantly, myself.

At the time, due to my eating disorder, many of my behaviors aligned with a type One, and that is what I originally tested as. But it became apparent that I was a type Eight when, as I read that chapter, tears pricked my eyes with each paragraph I read. I felt entirely known, seen, and understood.

Just like any journey, mine has had its fits and starts. But fast-forward sixteen years to today, and the Enneagram has been instrumental in my journey of recovery as well as my personal and spiritual growth, thanks in part to the work of Enneagram teachers and coaches like Elisabeth.

"Too much" were words I've felt deeply in my bones for as long as I can remember. I felt too much, I felt *like* too much, and, at times, I was even told that I *was* too much. As a type Eight, especially a female type Eight, I have felt profoundly misunderstood much of my life, which has served to compound this feeling of being "too much." Since my earliest childhood, I have felt a pulsating energy and underlying force to *go* and *do*. I still feel this energy and force in my body most days.

This passion and energy has left a wake of destruction behind me as I've barraged through life, careless and unaware of how my lust, drive, and anger affected others. It's been sobering to see the pain I've inflicted on people by my general unawareness. My living from a place where I allowed my sin tendency of lust to run amuck in my relationships, always wanting more and engaging in toxic cycles of conflict, only served to compound the feeling of being misunderstood.

Yet that same passion and energy propelled me to move abroad and work for a nonprofit organization, caring for the medical and surgical needs of orphan children, and help to establish a team of sexual-assault nurse examiners to serve victims of sexual assault and domestic violence in Nashville. It has further been the undercurrent and driving force behind my personal and spiritual growth that, by God's grace, has transformed me into a very different person than that fifteen-year-old girl who originally discovered her Enneagram type.

For type Eights, our strength is considerable, but our lust is our kryptonite. It's what renders us completely powerless and ineffective. It's in the quiet moments of surrender and vulnerability that our strength lies instead. It's in moments of stillness where our ability to bring about change and establish justice is found. That's what this journey has illuminated for me, and it's the beckoning call I wake up to each day. Luke 9:23 speaks of that call: *"And he said to all, 'If anyone would come after me, let him deny himself and take up his cross daily and follow me.'"* We're called to deny ourselves the lust of the flesh and the vengeance that, to a type Eight, seems impossible to leave to God. (See Deuteronomy 32:35; Romans 12:19.)

Will we find the stillness our bodies, hearts, and minds need to act and respond appropriately? Will we surrender to our softer side and lean into vulnerability? Having been washed in the redeeming blood of Jesus Christ, we can confidently answer the way the apostle Paul does in Galatians 2:20: *"I have been crucified with Christ. It is no longer I who live, but Christ who lives in me. And the life I now live in the flesh I live by faith in the Son of God, who loved me and gave himself for me."* Having died with him to the lust of our flesh, we are able to find the stillness our busy bodies and frenzied hearts desperately need and surrender to the work being done in our souls through vulnerability.

The next sixty days in the pages of this book will be transformational if you are willing to lean into the work the Holy Spirit is doing in your heart. The words written and Scripture references can pierce through even the toughest exterior into the innermost places of your soul. This book will serve as a guide for uncovering the tenderness that lives just beneath the surface but easily gets pushed down with anger; it will guide you to harness your energy and passion so that you are not mindlessly and carelessly blitzing through life, unintentionally taking out anyone and anything in your path. And it will show you how you can uniquely reflect the image of God through your natural leadership and gift of strength.

Here is your guide; this is your invitation. Lean in, my friend. Dig into the work. The journey is not for the faint of heart, but, thankfully, you have the strength it will require. You may very well still feel misunderstood at times, but you will come to know others more deeply, finding connection and belonging, and you will be known by others when you choose vulnerability. The reward that awaits is worth every challenge and every moment of surrender this journey requires.

I cannot wait for you to reap the reward that lies ahead and experience the joy and purpose found in living in the unique Eight-ness of who you were created to be.

—*Meredith Boggs*
The Other Half Podcast

ACKNOWLEDGMENTS

My journey from young hopeful writer, all the way back to the tender age of four, to holding books with my name on them hasn't been easy or pretty. In fact, it's held a lot of hurt, disappointment, and rejection. However, as you hold a book with my name on the cover in your hands, I'd love you to know who and what has sustained me through it all. You are holding a piece of God's redemption in my story, tangible proof of His kindness, and testament of His faithfulness. I didn't break any doors down or *do* anything myself that ensured my trajectory of publishing. God in His kindness handed me this opportunity, and to Him alone belongs all the glory and praise.

My agent Amanda deserves the highest of thanks and admiration. Thank you for answering my many questions, guiding me, and giving me the confidence to do this. I couldn't have done it without you. To all the people at Whitaker House, my editor Peg and publisher Christine, thank you for making these devotionals what they are today. It's been a pleasure working with you all.

Christine Rollings, thank you for your faithful work on this project and your encouragement. You have been a joy, as always. I am so grateful for you.

To my writing community hope*writers, thank you for giving me the courage to call myself a writer long before I felt like one. To Meredith Boggs, I'm so grateful you wrote the foreword for this devotional and are a friend in the Enneagram world. You are doing big things for God's kingdom!

Thank you to Pastor Bubba Jennings at Resurrection Church for reading over my proposal and giving me advice on how to serve Jesus well in this process.

The people who have been the biggest support and help to me during the process of writing this devotional for Eights are:

Connie Miller, I am so grateful you are part of my family and trusted me to help you find your Enneagram type. You are strong, bold, thoughtful, and so very supportive. I thank God often for our Aunt Connie!

Tracy Mann, thank you for leading @8ish_andIknowit with such passion and care. You have taught me so much about Eights!

Carrie Givens, I am just *so* grateful I was introduced to you through Christine and you agreed to share your wisdom, talents, and heart with your fellow Eights. I know your words will help many Eights feel less alone.

Dave Harris, I remember the first time Peter told me he thought you were an Eight, and I bristled. I have struggled with a lot of Eights in my life and have felt misunderstood on several occasions, especially online. The more I thought about you being an Eight, God slowly used your example to redeem what Eights had to be in my mind. By the time you confirmed that you were, in fact, an Eight, I was able to give God all the praise for softening my heart toward Eights and giving me such an impactful example in you. You will forever be one of the biggest influences in my early adulthood, and I am so grateful for how God has used you in my life. Thank you for sharing your wisdom in these pages! I hope your encouragement to be a tender parent and spouse leads many weary eyes to be fixed on Christ.

To all the other Eights in my life who have left a big impact on me: Danielle Bate, Sidney Stanislaw, Shaina Beil, HaleyJo Swinscoe, all of my Enneagram Eight clients, and a couple of other suspected Eights whom I won't publicly "type" here. Thank you!

Sarah Upton, I can't even articulate all the thankfulness I feel in my heart for the best little sister in the world. I am a lucky recipient of God's work in your life, and I am so grateful for how you love us.

John and Jan Bennett, thank you for faithfully praying for me and supporting me through this entire process. Your encouragement has moved mountains and sustained me on the hardest days.

Mom and Dad (Joe and Diane Upton), thank you for literally teaching me to read and write and encouraging me to say yes to big things. I would never have had the foundation to say yes without you and how you raised me. I'm so proud and grateful to have the two of you in my corner cheering me on.

Peter, you've been beyond supporting, patient, and caring toward me. I don't know what else I would've expected from a One. You have taught me so much about what it means to be faithful, and you never let me quit. You believe in me enough for both of us, and I can't believe the gift that you are in my life. You're my best friend, and I love you.

INTRODUCTION
What Is the Enneagram?

The Enneagram is an ancient personality typology for which no one really knows the origins.

It uses nine points within a circle—the word itself means "a drawing of nine"—to represent nine distinct personality types. The points are numbered simply to differentiate between them, with each point having no greater or less value than the others. The theory is that a person assumes one of these personalities in childhood as a reaction to discovering that the world is a scary, unkind place that is unlikely to accept their true self.

The nine types are identified by their numbers or by these names:

1. The Perfectionist
2. The Helper
3. The Achiever
4. The Individualist
5. The Thinker
6. The Guardian
7. The Enthusiast
8. The Challenger
9. The Peacemaker

HOW DO I FIND MY TYPE?

Your Enneagram type is determined by your main motivation. Finding your type is a journey, as we are typically unaware of our motivations and instead focus on our behaviors. Many online tests focus on behaviors, and while some motivations *may* produce certain behaviors, this may not always be the case, and you are unlikely to get accurate results.

To find your Enneagram type, you need to start by learning about *all* nine Enneagram types and exploring their motivations in contrast to your own behaviors and deeper motivations.

You can ask for feedback from those around you, but most often, the more you learn, the clearer your core number shines through.

It's often the number whose description makes you feel the most *exposed* that is your true core type. Your core Enneagram number won't change, since it's solidified in childhood.

Each number's distinct motivation:

1. Integrity – Goodness

2. Love – Relationships

3. Worth – Self-Importance

4. Authenticity – Unique Identity

5. Competency – Objective Truth

6. Security – Guidance

7. Satisfaction – Freedom

8. Independence – Control

9. Peace – Equilibrium

IS THIS JOURNEY WORTH IT?

Yes! The self-awareness you gain along the way is gold, and learning about the other types in the process brings you so much empathy and understanding for all the other personalities in your life.

WHAT MAKES THE ENNEAGRAM UNIQUE AND DIFFERENT FROM MYERS-BRIGGS, STRENGTHSFINDER, OR DISC ASSESSMENTS?

Unlike other typology systems, the Enneagram is fluid. Yes, the Enneagram tells you what your base personality characteristics are, but it also reveals how you change when you're growing, stressed, secure, unhealthy, healthy, etc.

You are not the same person at twenty as you are at sixty. You're not the same person at your stressful workplace as you are when binge-watching your favorite TV show and eating ice cream at home. The Enneagram accounts for these inconsistencies and changes in our behavior and informs you of when and how those changes occur.

If you look at the following graph, you'll see that each of the numbers connects to two other numbers by arrows. The arrow pointed toward your number is your growth arrow; the arrow pointed away is your stress number. When your life leaves you with more room to breathe, you exhibit the positive characteristics of your growth number, and when you're stretched thin in seasons of stress, you exhibit the negative characteristics of your stress number.

This is one explanation for big shifts in personality over a lifetime.

Another point of difference between the Enneagram and other typology systems is *wings*. Your wings are the two numbers on either side of your core number, which add flavor to your personality type. Although your core number won't change—and your main motivation, sin proclivities, and personality will come from that core number—your wings can be very influential on your overall personality and how it

presents itself. There are many different theories about wings, but the viewpoint we hold to is:

+ Your wing can only be one of the two numbers on either side of your core number. Therefore, you can be an 8 with a 7 wing (8w7) but not an 8 with a 6 wing (8w6).

+ You have access to the numbers on either side of your number, but most people will only have one dominant wing. (*Dominant* meaning you exhibit more of the behaviors of one wing than the other wing.) It is possible to have equal wings or no wing at all, but this is rare.

+ Your dominant wing number can change from one to the other throughout your life, but it's speculated this might only happen once.

As you read through this book, we will go over what an Enneagram Eight looks like with both of its wings. If you're struggling to figure out what your core number is, this book series could really help give you some more in-depth options!

HOW DO YOU BECOME YOUR TYPE?

Personality is a kind of shield we pick up, and hide behind. It is functional, even protective at times, but altogether unnecessary because God made us in His image from the start. However, we cling to this personality like it's our key to survival, and nothing has proved us wrong so far. It's the only tool we've ever had, and the shield has scratches and dents to prove its worth.

Not all parts of our personality are wrong or bad, but by living in a fallen, sinful world, we all tend to distort even good things in bad ways. Amen?

What personality did you pick up in childhood? If you're reading this devotional, then you may have chosen type Eight. Your need to be independent became the one thing that your life would rotate around from early in childhood up until right now, at this very moment.

The Enneagram talks about childhood wounds and how we pick up a particular shield as a reaction to these wounds.

However, not all siblings have the same Enneagram type even though they heard the same wounding message or had the same harmful experiences growing up. This is because we are born with our own unique outlook on the world, and we filter everything through that outlook. You and your siblings may have heard the same things, but while you heard, "You can only trust yourself," your sister might have heard, "You're only loved when you're successful." Thus, you both would become different Enneagram types.

Trauma and abuse of all kinds can definitely impact your choice of shield as well. If you think of all these nine shields as being a different color, perhaps you were born predisposed to be more likely to pick blue than red. However, in a moment of early trauma, you might have heard someone shouting, "Pick black! Black is the only option!" Thus, you chose black instead of blue, which would've been your own unique reaction to your life circumstances. It's hard to say how these things happen exactly, especially when trauma is involved. Are you who you are *despite* trauma...or because of it? Only God knows, but there is healing and growth to be found either way.

We've all heard the phrase, "You can't teach an old dog new tricks." I'd like to propose that when referencing personality, it might be said, "The longer you use your personality, the harder it is to see its ineffectiveness." It's not impossible for an older person to drastically change for the better, but it will be harder for them to put down what has worked for them for so long. That's why, as we age, it can become harder to even see where our personality ends and our true self begins. Even if the unhealthy parts of our personality have been ineffective, they still seem to be the only things that have worked for us.

WHY DO WE NEED THE ENNEAGRAM WHEN WE HAVE THE HOLY SPIRIT AND THE BIBLE TO GUIDE US?

The Enneagram is a helpful tool, but only when it is used as such. The Enneagram cannot save you—only Jesus can do that. However, God made us all unique, and we all reflect Him in individual ways. Learning about these unique reflections can encourage us, as well as point us toward our purposes. The Enneagram also reveals the sin problems and blind spots of each type with which you may unknowingly struggle. Revealing these can lead us to repentance and change before God..

HOW DO I CHANGE MY MORE NEGATIVE BEHAVIORS?

Alcoholics Anonymous was really on to something when they called their first step "admitting you have a problem." How do you solve a problem if you don't know you have one or are in denial about it? You can't. If you have a shield you're using to protect yourself from the world, but are blissfully unaware of its existence, you won't understand how its very existence impacts you and your relationships. You definitely won't be putting that battered but battle-tested shield of a personality down anytime soon.

Similar to the wisdom of admitting one has a problem before recovery can begin, the Enneagram proposes self-knowledge as the starting point before there can be change.

Whether you're 100 percent sure you are an Enneagram Eight, or just curious about the possibility, this is what it looks like to be an Eight.

WHAT IT MEANS TO BE A CHALLENGER

Eights are the only Enneagram type that you can literally feel walk into a room. They are the football coach with confidence for days, the boss whose very presence inspires everyone to sit a little straighter, and a friend who has the softest heart yet intimidates most people until they get to know her.

Eights aren't called the Challenger for nothing. With an energy and confidence about them that few can beat, an Eight won't shy away from a verbal spar. In fact, they'll often drop a controversial bomb on a conversation just to stir things up and see if anyone has the guts to stand up to them. Eights can also be known as the Advocate because of their fire for justice and standing up for the underdog. Wherever there's a protest against ill treatment, you'll probably find more than a handful of Eights shouting the loudest.

Danielle learned at a very young age that she needed to rely on herself. When she was less than two years old, her mother was put on bed rest while pregnant with her sister. Her mom would direct Danielle to go get her own diapers and come back to the bed to be changed. Even at that young age, Danielle had some level of responsibility for herself. And it's fair to say that left an impression on her.

As a child, Danielle had confidence for days. Around age six or seven, she decided that she wanted to have a party. So she went to the grocery store that her family owned at the time and picked out all of her favorite things; she then proceeded to phone her guest list, which consisted of adult employees at the store, a group of her uncle's buddies, and her parents—not a single child! Danielle's confidence made her think of herself as equal to adults and children alike.

If Danielle's family had known about the Enneagram back then, they wouldn't have been surprised to see the confidence, energy, and independence she was coming into. Learning about the Enneagram as an adult has been life changing for her. She has been able to see her Eight-ness as a gift and learn that she doesn't have to change herself to be sensitive to others, although she may need to let people catch up to her full sprint speed of life a little. She can be fully herself and understand that not everyone sees the world through her confidence and anything-is-possible energy.

Healthy Eights are confident, energetic, and assertive, but there's tangible compassion about the way they listen to and care for others. These Eights use their strength to protect others and they often champion the underdogs in society.

At their most healthy, Eights will more easily embrace the emotions they feel and not discount emotions in themselves or others as weakness.

Average or slightly unhealthy Eights will easily mow over others even when they aren't trying to. Not wanting to be controlled, they often jump into leadership roles and lose respect for people who don't pull their weight. These Eights will use conflict as a way of testing whether others are worthy of respect; often they do not give compassion or grace to those who are not like them.

Unhealthy Eights may struggle with delusions of power and seem to forget their own mortality. Flying off the handle when they feel disrespected, these Eights have very little patience or compassion for others.

ALL ABOUT BEING AN EIGHT

MOTIVATION

Independence or Autonomy

Eights desire to be in control of themselves and to be free from the control of others.

BIGGEST FEAR

Being Betrayed

Eights fear being betrayed, especially by those they trust most.

GUT TRIAD

Each Enneagram type is dominant in either feeling, thinking, or doing. These *triads* are referred to as heart-centered, head-centered, and gut-centered.

Eights, along with Ones and Nines, are considered to be part of the gut triad. This means that they receive information through their gut, which in layman's terms means a bodily feeling of something being instinctively right or wrong. A person who has a dominant gut instinct doesn't need to think something over or consult their feelings in order to know what is right. This gut instinct is something unique to these three numbers, and dominance in this instinct is something only they experience.

Each of the three triads has a defining emotion connected to the center they use most. For the gut triad, this emotion is anger. Anger is like a fire that keeps this triad going, whether they're aware of it or not. Eights, Ones, and Nines struggle with anger, usually over the things that to them are obviously right or wrong. Injustice, marginalization, bullying, and a host of other issues that come from living in a sinful world are more than enough for this triad to struggle with persistent anger, especially as they receive all this information through their gut. To these types, the obvious right and wrong can't be put out of sight logically (through the head) or emotionally (through the heart).

CHILDHOOD WOUND

The wounding message young Eights heard (or thought they heard) was, "It is not okay to be vulnerable or to trust anyone," or "You can only trust yourself." This message causes Eights to take their security into their own hands and fight off (sometimes literally) anything or anyone that may want to control them. Eights become very protective of both themselves and the ones they love. They trust only a few, and even with those few, they can find it difficult to be totally open or vulnerable.

An Eight might've heard this message if their parent or guardian failed in some big way, thus making the Eight feel betrayed or scared, or if they said, "You can only trust yourself," or "The world is a scary place," or "Never trust a man/woman! You'll only get hurt."

THE LOST CHILDHOOD MESSAGE EIGHTS LONG TO HEAR

"You will not be betrayed."

Eights long to hear the message, "You will not be betrayed." Only God can speak these words to your soul and have them be true—and He does! In Joshua 1:5, He says, *"I will not leave you or forsake you."* You have a God who is 100 percent trustworthy, even when everyone else might not be. Trust Him with your softness, and He'll help you trust others as well.

DEFENSE MECHANISM

Denial

Denial is the defense mechanism Eights employ when they're stress, defensive, or otherwise need to protect themselves. It's theorized that Eights can get so caught up in denying the things that hurt them that they can even forget the name of a former best friend.

Denial is a front, it's a mind game, and it's all an act designed to protect Eights from feeling hurt.

WINGS

A wing is one of the numbers on either side of your Enneagram number that adds some *flavor* to your type. You'll still be your core number in essence, but your wing can impact a lot of your behaviors.

Eight with a Seven Wing (8w7)

An Eight with a Seven wing is said to be the highest energy number on the Enneagram. Combining an Eight's intensity with the go-go-go of a Seven results in a high energy, fun, and sometimes intimidating number. Eights with a Seven wing can often perceive any indecisiveness as a request for leadership, and they're happy to step into that role. More social than your average wingless Eight (or 8w9), the 8w7 has a hard time saying no to the promise of enjoyment, making them somewhat reckless when immature.

Their inner tension is between their core number's need to be seen as strong and respectful and their wing's need to be spontaneous and carefree. Obviously, these two needs can coexist, but respect brings with it a lot of responsibility that can make a freedom-loving wing a bit antsy.

Eight with a Nine Wing (8w9)

An Eight with a Nine wing may seem like an odd number combo: a Challenger with a Peacemaker wing. They're pleasant unless you cross them or someone they care about. If you do that, an 8w9 is likely to go into fierce protector mode. The Enneagram Institute aptly named this wing combo "The Bear," reflecting their role as the ultimate boundary keeper and protector. Quieter than the average Eight (or 8w7), an 8w9 is usually an introvert or ambivert. While they keep mostly to themselves, Eights with a Nine wing will show you a completely different side when they find an injustice they can do something to fix; in fact, in times like that, they'll talk your ear off about a cause they're passionate about.

The tension for an 8w9 lies between keeping the harmony, but still needing to be in control of what they find most important, often keeping others safe or not letting incompetence control them.

ARROWS

The arrows are the two numbers your Enneagram number is connected to in the Enneagram diagram. These two arrows represent the number from which you get the best traits as you grow or the number from which you get the worst traits when you're in seasons of stress.

Stress: Going to Five

In stress, normally energetic Eights will slow down and even withdraw as they act out like unhealthy Fives. Eights will become disengaged, more emotionally unaware, and suspicious of betrayal as they become stressed.

Growth: Going to Two

In growth, tough Eights become softer and more personable as they pick up the healthy behaviors of Twos. As Eights feel secure, they're more likely to listen, care for others' needs, and let their emotional side show without fear of losing control or respect.

TYPE EIGHT SUBTYPES

When we talk about subtypes and the Enneagram, we are referring to three relational instincts we all have. These instincts, like those of *fight or flight*, are reactions over which we have little control. The three relational subtypes are Self-Preservation (Sp), Social (So), and One-to-One (Sx). We all have the capacity to use all three of these instincts, but one of them is usually dominant. That dominant subtype can strongly impact how your distinct Enneagram type looks to the rest of us.

The "Protective" Eight (Sp)

Eights with a dominant Self-Preservation subtype will be drawn to those who are weak or hurting. They often effortlessly slip into a mother or father role. This subtype comes off as strong, confident, and very resilient. They don't tolerate nonsense or ill treatment from others and make difficult decisions without wasting any time. From the outside, this subtype can seem cold, but their very warm and tender heart is on full display to those they nurture. This subtype of Eight is the least likely to mistype.

The "Sacrificial" Eight (So)

Dominant Social Eights will appear to be much more focused on others than the other two subtypes. Being the countertype, these Eights aren't as preoccupied with power or strength. They want to protect, serve, and help those they care about. Usually, whole people groups—an organization, workplace, or family—are in these Eights' bracket of needing to be helped and protected. Social Eights focus a lot of their mental energy on fixing the mistreatment they notice around them. This is the Eight subtype that looks the most like a Two.

The "Reckless" Eight (Sx)

One-to-One subtype Eights could be best described as rebels. At some point, they found truth to be contrary to what most people passively believe, and they may have felt a deep betrayal. This subtype believes that by being open or loud in their rebellion, people will notice and change. These Eights can look a lot like Fours because their passion is loud and they may come across as highly emotional.

SO I'M A EIGHT. WHAT NOW?

Why should I, as a type Eight, embark on sixty days of devotions?

Whether you have just realized you are a type Eight on the Enneagram or have come to terms with that reality, you've probably thought at one point or another, *Okay, but what now? I get that I'm a challenger, I'm protective, it can be hard for me to trust people, I value being seen as strong, and others cannot control me. The question is, how do I take this self-awareness and turn it into practical transformation?*

Some Enneagram teachers will tell you that you need only to focus on self-actualization and pull yourself up by your proverbial bootstraps to grow out of your worst behaviors. They say things like, "Meditate!" or "Focus on yourself!" or "Stop being too much!"

However, I'm here to offer a different foundation for growth. As Christians, we know that we are flawed, sinful, and far away from God's intended plan for humanity. The hymn "Come Thou Fount of Every Blessing" includes the lyrics, "Prone to wander, Lord, I feel it." This speaks to the reality of our hearts and their rebellious nature toward our Savior.

This wandering is the problem, sin is the problem, and we are the problem! So, anyone who tells us that we ought to focus on ourselves to find growth will only lead us to more confusion. We may even find ourselves back where we started, as we go around and around this idea of focusing on self.

But we are not without hope. Philippians 1:6 says: *"I am sure of this, that he who began a good work in you will bring it to completion at the day of Jesus Christ."* On the very day you acknowledged Jesus as your Savior, repented from your sin, and dedicated your life to Him, He began a good work in your life. This work is called sanctification, which is the act of becoming holy. Your sanctification will not be finished here on earth, but you are in the process of becoming, day by day, moment by moment, only by the Holy Spirit's work and power within you.

We might not know how to articulate it, but this work of sanctification is the growth and change for which we long. All of us know we are not who we want to be. Reflecting on the human condition in Romans 7:15, Paul said, *"For I do not understand my own actions. For I do not do what I want, but I do the very thing I hate."* Isn't that the truth? I don't want to be angry, but in a world full of flaws, my anger has marked more days than I care to share.

We all know we have this haunting *potential* that always seems just a little out of reach. We all have this nagging feeling that we are created for more...but how do we get there? Only by God's grace and power within us can we rest in His sanctifying work and trust Him for the growth and potential of bringing glory to Him day by day. Only God can sanctify us, but it is our responsibility to be *"slaves to righteousness"* (Romans 6:18) and obey Him.

Over the next sixty days, we want to take you day by day through what God says about *your specific problems as an Eight* and how He wants to lovingly sanctify you into being more like Jesus.

The lens of the Enneagram gives us a great starting point for your specific pain points and strengths. We will use those to encourage you in the areas that God is reflected through you and in the areas that you need to lay down your instincts and let Him change you.

Some of these topics might be hard, but we hope that you'll let the tension you feel in your heart open you up to change. This is where our obedience comes in. We all have blind spots and areas we are more comfortable leaving in the dark, but God desires so much more for us. So ask Him to help you release your grip on those areas, bring them into the light, and experience the freedom of repentance.

Always have to be big and bold

No matter what's going on inside my own soul

Just because you never see the scared, the soft, the quiet

Doesn't mean I never feel it; it just feels too private

Inside I still feel the things that you feel

Even if I'm not ready to be real

I take it as a badge of honor, to be your protector and confidant

Please always remember that I care a LOT

How are you doing? How heavy is the load?

Things people don't think to ask, because I've always got things under control

If you ask and I say nothing, if I don't open up

Just remember I still noted, that you cared enough

—*Danielle Bate*

YOUR GUIDES FOR THIS JOURNEY

You'll be hearing from three other writers and Enneagram coaches in the days ahead. The days in which no author is listed are written by me. On other days, I have asked two Enneagram Eights and a fellow Enneagram enthusiast to help you on your path.

CAROLYN CLARE GIVENS

An Eight with a Nine wing, Carolyn is a displaced Northerner exploring the foreign ways of the South. She works in communications and the arts at New City Church in North Carolina, does freelance editing and writing, and is one of the founders of Bandersnatch Books. Carrie lives in Charlotte with her two literary cats, Lord Peter Wimsey and Harriet Vane. She has previously bumped around the world, both as a missionary kid and an adult. Fiction is her first love, and Carrie is the author of *The King's Messenger*, a chapter book for ages eight to eleven, and *Rosefire*, a young adult fantasy novel.

ALISON BRADLEY

Alison is an Enneagram Nine who has always loved stories, whether it is reading them or helping others listen to their own. You'll often find her outside making a bouquet of flowers, or inside relaxing at the local library. She also loves being around her kitchen table in Bucks County, Pennsylvania, with her husband and two kids, often eating gluten-free chocolate chip pancakes.

CHRISTINE ROLLINGS

Christine is an Enneagram Two with a desire to help people understand themselves and have the words to express their story to others. After finding the Enneagram helpful for naming her own strengths, longings, and struggles, she was led to become an Enneagram coach. She works particularly with people living cross-culturally, with their particular set of challenges and joys. Having her stress arrow pointing toward type Eight not only gives her a depth of understanding of Eights' pain points, but also a lot of insight into Eights going to Two in growth.

DAVE HARRIS

Dave is an Eight with a Seven wing. He married his high school sweetheart, is a father, and serves in vocational ministry. Dave began studying the Enneagram as a tool for understanding himself and others. He has found it to be instrumental in learning how others think and how motives are important. As an Eight, this means learning daily how to be vulnerable and let people see the softer side of a hard exterior personality. His hope, as a Christian, husband, father, brother, and leader, is that we may all grow in Christ, understanding that He is central and we, as many diverse members of His body, play an integral role in the kingdom.

10 DAYS OF STRENGTH

How You Uniquely Reflect God

• • • • • • • • • • **DAY 1**

How We All Reflect God

And let the peace of Christ rule in your hearts,
to which indeed you were called in one body.
(Colossians 3:15)

Dear Challenger, do you know you uniquely reflect God? In Genesis, God says that He made us in His image. Now, this doesn't mean our bodies look like His, but rather that we reflect His image by reflecting parts of God's character. It's not a perfect reflection; in fact, it's rippled and marred. However, a familiarity, a family resemblance, is still plainly evident between God and His creation.

God is so mighty, majestic, and perfect that none of us can reflect every part of Him, so we see His attributes scattered throughout the entire population. Each of us is reflecting Him in unique and very important ways. This is why we hear about each of us being a part of God's body in Scriptures such as 1 Corinthians 12:27, Romans 12:5, and Ephesians 5:30. Each of us is uniquely made for a divine purpose; each of us would be lost without the others.

As an Eight, you reflect God's strength, His vigilance, His zeal, His inspiring nature, and His protective heart toward us. God made you uniquely, specifically, and purposefully. Your strength might protect you and those you love, but it ultimately is given to you to reflect God.

Your desire to see justice served, how you seek truth, and your tendency toward action may feel second nature to you as an Eight, especially as you are following Christ. But these are all important ways you uniquely reflect God to those around you.

SHIFT IN FOCUS

Did you grow up hearing about a physical resemblance you shared with someone else? Similar quirks? As you go about your day, invite God to reveal the ways He's made you to look like Him. If you have space, pull out a journal and think of things you've noticed about yourself or heard others say about your drive, excellence, inspiring, encouraging, or understanding.

God can help you notice these parts of who you are. Thank Him for choosing you and calling you holy and beloved. Invite Him to continue to grow you as a Challenger who looks like Him.

• • • • • • • • • • • **DAY 2**

How Eights Reflect God

> *The LORD is my strength and my shield*
> *in him my heart trusts, and I am helped;*
> *my heart exults, and with my song*
> *I give thanks to him.*
> (Psalm 28:7)

The traditional virtue of Eights is strength, but not just in the physical sense (although a lot of Eights are physically strong). The strength that God provides and that Eights reflect is psychological, emotional, *and* physical, with the stamina to protect others. Strength is something we see in the Bible that God provides, and Eights' strength is a reflection of our strong God. This strength gives Eights the natural drive and responsibility to be protectors of those who are hurt, weak, or in danger. I can imagine God rushing into battle with Eights by His side, knowing they'll fight as He does for the protection of those who can't.

Here are some other ways that Eights reflect God:

+ *Vigilance.* Eights are realistic about the need for vigilance in everyday life. This protective, cautious, and fact-checking energy is a sign of them knowing the responsibility they carry. When Eights are healthy, this characteristic is reflective of God's watchful eye over His children. Vigilance may be described as keeping careful watch for possible danger or difficulty. In 1 Peter 5:8, God tells us to be vigilant against Satan:

"Be sober-minded; be watchful. Your adversary the devil prowls around like a roaring lion seeking someone to devour."

+ *Justice.* Eights have a naturally strong sense of justice. They see the wrong, evil, and horrible things happening in the world around them, and their very soul is angered and demands justice. This is a reflection of God's own heart for justice, for He will carry out His perfect justice in the end.

+ *Zeal or passion.* This radiates from most Eights. They can't help it. And when they're healthy, this zeal is pointed in the right direction, which is toward God. Romans 12:11 says: *"Do not be slothful in zeal, be fervent in spirit, serve the Lord."*

+ *Tenderness.* This refers to gentleness or kindness marked by sensitivity to pain. This might be a surprising word to see for Eights, but it describes them well. Especially when Eights are healthy and growing, they have very tender hearts toward the weak and hurting.

SHIFT IN FOCUS

How in your life has God shown Himself to be strong?

Which of these attributes were you surprised to see named as a way you reflect God?

Which attribute is your favorite?

• • • • • • • • • • • **DAY 3**

Eights' Natural Strength

As each has received a gift, use it to serve one another,
as good stewards of God's varied grace.
(1 Peter 4:10)

When was the first time you noticed your strength? Maybe you've never called yourself strong but others have. Or maybe you don't notice your own strength, but you notice the weakness in others. However your strength appears for you, there is no denying that strength is a natural gifting for type Eights.

This strength is not always physical. Some Eights are small in stature and not very strong physically (although a lot of them are). However, there's a toughness that comes with being an Eight. This toughness centers on your need for independence. When you won't be controlled, you tend to carry yourself in a way that speaks to that: "Don't tread on me," you seem to proclaim.

This is not something that you can turn on or off; it is just a way of being. Eights have a strong presence that many people don't have a word for other than *intimidating*—but we'll get to that later.

Some Eights are aware of this presence and use it to their advantage. But the vast majority of Eights are go-with-the-flow people until they smell a rat, someone tries to take advantage of another, or they're challenged. I once heard that you only have to do something once a month for those around you to expect you to repeat that behavior at any time. This is the sense that others get from Eights. They're ready for you to go into protection mode at any time because you can and you will if needed.

This is where you see Eights' strength truly shine: when they're using it to expose, protect, and defend. You are the natural protectors God has given to the world, and although it's a thankless, never-ending job, you're well suited for it.

You have a strength that runs to your core, you have an energy that won't stop until your body gives out, and you care deeply about the weak and hurting.

Unlike the other Enneagram types, this strength comes naturally to you.

SHIFT IN FOCUS

Do you view your strength as a good gift?

How does your God-given strength help you serve others?

Do you ever struggle to see yourself as strong?

• • • • • • • • • • • • DAY 4

God's Strength
By Carolyn Clare Givens

Ascribe power to God, whose majesty is over Israel, and whose
power is in the skies. Awesome is God from his sanctuary;
the God of Israel—he is the one who gives power and
strength to his people. Blessed be God!
(Psalm 68:34–35)

Dear Challenger, God is stronger than you are. I know you know that. But do you know it in a deep, sinks-into-your-bones, anchor-of-your-soul way?

The apostle Paul, in writing to the church at Corinth, talks about boasting. He says he just can't stop it. And what is he boasting about? God's strength. God's work. He says, *"On my own behalf I will not boast, except of my weaknesses"* (2 Corinthians 12:5), and then he goes on to point out that he could boast of his strengths. The guy was a big deal. He was a leader among the Pharisees at a young age and his pedigree was impeccable. (See Philippians 3:4–6.)

Once Jesus took hold of Paul's heart, he still was successful in almost everything he put his hand to. Indeed, Paul calls himself the hardest working apostle. (See 1 Corinthians 15:10.)

But then he says this:

So to keep me from becoming conceited because of the sur-
passing greatness of the revelations, a thorn was given me in

the flesh, a messenger of Satan to harass me, to keep me from becoming conceited. Three times I pleaded with the Lord about this, that it should leave me. But he said to me, "My grace is sufficient for you, for my power is made perfect in weakness." (2 Corinthians 12:7–9)

We as Eights are often tempted to live out of our strength. We like that God made us able to withstand a lot—physically, emotionally, and mentally. But we can never forget that *"he is the one who gives power and strength to his people"* (Psalm 68:35). All our strengths are counted as weaknesses without God lifting us up and sustaining us.

"Ascribe power to God," the psalmist commands. So, I say it once more: God is stronger than I am.

SHIFT IN FOCUS

Do you find it hard to accept—deep down in your bones—that you are weak and God is strong? How can you lean into that truth today?

Where can you lean on Him for strength today?

• • • • • • • • • • • DAY 5

What the Bible Says about Strength
By Carolyn Clare Givens

As each has received a gift, use it to serve one another, as good stewards of God's varied grace: whoever speaks, as one who speaks oracles of God; whoever serves, as one who serves by the strength that God supplies—in order that in everything God may be glorified through Jesus Christ. To him belong glory and dominion forever and ever. Amen. (1 Peter 4:10–11)

What are your gifts? I'm not asking you to take a spiritual gifts test and write down your answers here. What I'm asking is: what are you good at? What are your strengths? In what areas do you thrive when you contribute to your family, friends, or church?

Eights are often the strong ones in a group. We're the active contributors, and we keep things rolling along. We have leadership gifts, and what we may lack in empathy or perspective we make up for in efficiency and determination—which isn't actually the best thing.

In today's Scripture reading, the apostle Peter reminds the dispersed believers that they are merely stewards of the gifts God has given to them. So, therefore, those gifts are made to serve, not to empower themselves. And whoever serves, he says, should do so with the strength God provides.

Just as God is the source of life itself, just as from Him, through Him, and to Him are all things (Romans 11:36), He is the source of all strength. We are stewards of it.

In the days when there were far more monarchs and noblemen than we have today, the role of a steward was more familiar. He was the regent in his lord's place over the household or estate. He worked in the name of the lord and was empowered to make decisions up to a point, but only under the oversight of the nobleman.

The steward's authority and strength—his exercise of that authority—were provided entirely by his lord, just as our strength's source is entirely from *our* Lord, Jesus Christ.

SHIFT IN FOCUS

Pray that the Lord will show you how you can exercise His strength today. If these words reflect your heart, please use them:

Dear heavenly Father, help me to rely on You for my strength today. Remind me over and over again that You are the source of all the power I have. Make me a steward of Your gift, rather than one who wields strength just to flex it or to gain more. Make my contributions to those around me come from You. Amen.

• • • • • • • • • • •   **DAY 6**

Eights' Attraction to Strength
By Carolyn Clare Givens

I love you, O LORD, my strength. The LORD is my rock and my
fortress and my deliverer, my God, my rock, in whom I take refuge,
my shield, and the horn of my salvation, my stronghold.
(Psalm 18:1–2)

Dear Challenger, do you find yourself drawn to the passages of
Scripture that talk about God's strength? I do. Give me a verse
about God as a fortress any day of the week.

Strength is attractive. It's something to take hold of and be
lifted by. It's something to push up against and test our mettle.
It's something to lean against when we just can't hold ourselves
up any longer.

I've often said that, in friendships or other relationships, I'm
looking for a person who will fight me back. I don't *like* always
bowling everyone down. I don't *want* to always be the strong one.
I don't *need* to always be in charge. In fact, when I realize that
there is someone else in the room whom I can trust to capably
take charge of the situation, I usually feel like a huge weight is
taken off my chest.

It's not like this is easy, of course, even when the strong one
we're facing is God Himself. We do have a tendency to try to
wrestle back control, or—like Jacob at Jabbok (see Genesis
32:22–32)—hold on even when we know we're beaten and
demand that God bless us.

The strength we find so attractive is both exhilarating and restful. We can spar with it and feel the iron sharpening our own iron. (See Proverbs 27:17.) We can come to it and find rest when we are weary and burdened. (See Matthew 11:28.)

Do you find yourself more drawn to strength as a way to test your own strength or as a place to rest? Take a moment to consider your answer. It will say a lot about where you find yourself emotionally and physically.

SHIFT IN FOCUS

If you answered that you want to test your own strength, please use this prayer:

> Dear heavenly Father, I praise You for making me strong. When I'm striving with You, help me to remember that Your strength is *for* me. Remind me that all of my strength ultimately has its source in You and Your provision. Pour contempt on my pride, Lord, and forbid my boasting in anything except Your sacrifice on my behalf. Amen.

If you answered that you need a place to rest, please use this prayer:

> Dear heavenly Father, I thank You that I don't *have* to be the strong one with You. I'm so tired, Lord. You know the demands that I face every day. Please sustain me in them. Thank You for being my refuge. Thank You for accepting my weaknesses. Thank You for lifting me up.

Help me never to forget that You are always my *"refuge and strength, a very present help in trouble"* (Psalm 46:1). Amen.

DAY 7 • • • • • • • • • • •

A World That Needs Your Strength

For the LORD your God is he who goes
with you to fight for you against your
enemies, to give you the victory.
(Deuteronomy 20:4)

The world needs your strength—almost too much, if we're honest. There are never enough people fighting for the weak and defenseless. There are never enough soldiers, foster parents, advocates, or people who lay down their own comfort for the good of others. However, the people who do just this change the world.

As an Eight, you may be invigorated by the thought of advocacy, or you might be plain old tired of playing whack-a-mole with the problems of the world. I've seen both sides from Eights, and both are valid. Hearing that the world needs you might make you want to either roll your eyes or shout an "Amen!" But no matter what side of the fence you're sitting on, I want to remind you that the world doesn't need you; they need Jesus.

You can't solve the problems of the world on your own, and you were never meant to bear the weight of being some kind of pseudo-savior.

Your reflection of God is a powerful one. It's loud, and it's very public. But you are not God. The world needs you because they're longing to see God as a good, protective, caring, and advocating Father, and your reflection is part of that. You are the hands and feet of this particular aspect of God.

This is why one of the most powerful things you can do as an Eight is point others to Christ. Show them who they are really looking for. Use your gifts, and be generous with your strength, but don't let yourself become the savior that others look to.

Embolden others by showing them that God is the One who gives you your strength. They don't need to drain you when they can go straight to your source. Like Deuteronomy 20:4 says, the Lord will go with you and fight with you.

SHIFT IN FOCUS

Spend some time thanking God for your strength and asking for wisdom in how to use your strength to help a world starving for your gifts.

If these words reflect your heart, please borrow them:

Heavenly Father, I thank You that I do not need to be the savior the world is looking for because You already sent Your Son. I know You have already won this battle, but the work here is so vast and the needs are so many. Please give me wisdom in the way I protect and serve. Help me to point everyone back to You so that Your name would be glorified in every action I take that blesses someone. Amen.

DAY 8 • • • • • • • • • • •

Samson and Strength Stewarded

And Samson said, "Let me die with the Philistines." Then he bowed with all his strength, and the house fell upon the lords and upon all the people who were in it. So the dead whom he killed at his death were more than those whom he had killed during his life.
(Judges 16:30)

I have heard Eights say is that the book of Judges is their favorite book of the Bible. This is not surprising considering this is a book of action, strong people, and justice. The book of Judges covers the twelve leaders who were the judges of Israel before the institution of a monarchy. These judges led God's people and fought against the oppressors who surrounded them.

The final judge of Israel was named Samson, who was gifted with supernatural strength from God. Before Samson was even born, God had a purpose for him and had his parents set him aside as a Nazarite; this means he was not to drink wine, cut his hair, or have contact with a corpse. We tend to focus on the cutting of his hair as his only kryptonite, but if he had drunk wine or had contact with a corpse, he would have broken his Nazarite vow as well.

Samson stewarded his strength in the way that he protected God's people against the Philistines, but Samson was also reckless with his responsibility. We are told that Samson loved many foreign women, whom God had forbidden His people from marrying, and one of those women would betray him and lead to his downfall.

The Philistines were rightly scared of Samson and his great strength. They knew no bonds could hold him, and no cell could keep him. But Samson loved a prostitute named Delilah, so the Philistines bribed her to learn the source of Samson's strength.

And he told her all his heart, and said to her, "A razor has never come upon my head, for I have been a Nazirite to God from my mother's womb. If my head is shaved, then my strength will leave me, and I shall become weak and be like any other man." (Judges 16:17)

So Delilah cut his hair, and the Philistines captured him, gouged out his eyes, and bound him with shackles.

But God's plan for Samson was not thwarted by even his foolishness, sin, and mistakes. The Philistines put Samson on display in their heathen temple as they celebrated his capture. Bound between two pillars holding up the building, Samson prayed that God would strengthen him one last time. And as he leaned against the pillars, God came upon him and gave him great strength once more so that he could break the pillars and crush the Philistines in the temple. In his death, he killed more Philistines than he had in his lifetime.

Samson's sin and misuse of his life was not pleasing to God, but God used his folly for good, putting him in the right place at the right time to free his people from the Philistines.

SHIFT IN FOCUS

As you reflect on Samson's story, find encouragement in the fact that no matter how much you mess up, you cannot stop God's plan for your life. It may be less painful if you follow Him and are obedient to His commands, but even in pain, God will not waste what He has sown in you.

Read Judges 16.

• • • • • • • • • • • **DAY 9**

The Responsibility of Being Strong

*Everyone to whom much was given, of him much will be required,
and from him to whom they entrusted much, they will demand the
more. (Luke 12:48)*

Being strong is a gift, but it's also a responsibility. Just like power, money, and influence are responsibilities, having great strength isn't just a pass to do whatever you please with it. When your gifting is great, so is the responsibility placed on your shoulders.

Being responsible, in its purest form, means that someday you will have to answer for what you did with your strength. The Bible makes it clear that *"to whom much was given, of him much will be required"* (Luke 12:48). As we saw with Samson, when you have great strength, you also have many pairs of eyes watching you. Even if you do not desire to be a role model, as Christians, we all are. You're accountable to steward your gift as an image-bearer of God, and just like in the parable of the talents, your strength is a gift that should be used, not stored away and hidden.

Children are watching you, and they need you to role model what strength looks like when you're living in Christ. This is not something that is readily available to them in the media. Strong women and strong men, who can also be tender, are not always presented well or shown in their full godly strength. You can help shape the strong girls and boys who are growing up around you. A young Eight is very likely following your lead.

You can use strength to serve yourself, fill your heart with pride, and protect yourself. Or you can use your strength to serve others, fill a guardian role in the lives of those who don't have one, and speak for those who can't speak for themselves. Using your strength for others means getting attached, it means trusting, and it means opening yourself up to what might eventually be painful. These are the realities of living in a fallen world. But protecting yourself to avoid pain may be depriving others from witnessing God's reflection being lived out in you.

Sharing your gifts transforms your heart—which might be God's goal for you in your service in the first place. You're the only person you can control, and your obedience in stewarding your gift is what you're accountable for here, not others' response to it.

SHIFT IN FOCUS

Spend some time with God today, processing with Him what stewarding your strength looks like for you practically. You can do this by spending some quiet moments praying and journaling, or you can go for a run and talk to Him there, whichever is most effective for you.

Come back and write down one practical step you can take this week toward stewarding your strength:

• • • • • • • • • • • **DAY 10**

Glorifying God in Your Strength

The LORD is my strength and my song, and he has become my salvation; this is my God, and I will praise him, my father's God, and I will exalt him. (Exodus 15:2)

The Westminster Shorter Catechism states, "Man's chief end is to glorify God, and to enjoy him forever." [1] (See 1 Corinthians 10:31.)

We glorify God in our lives by giving Him the glory for everything He works through us. Our talents, our good deeds, our ability to love—everything good that comes from us is owed to God's work in our lives. This is what it means when people say, "*Soli Deo gloria*" or "Glory to God alone." Don't give the glory of my life to me, but instead look at anything worthy of praise in my life and give it to God; that's to whom it is owed.

To enjoy God forever means that after we glorify God in our lives, we then get to be in heaven with Him. This is our natural habitat; this is where all of our longing is fulfilled. This is our heart's cry: to be in a perfect relationship with our Father in heaven and enjoy His presence forever.

An abundant amount of your glorifying Christ, as an Eight, will involve your strength. When you lay down your own pride, comfort, and interests for others, people will want to praise

---

1. *The Westminster Shorter Catechism in Modern English* (Phillipsburg, NJ: Presbyterian and Reformed Pub. Co., 1986).

you—but you get the opportunity to glorify God instead of holding the glory for yourself.

You see, we are not meant to hold glory. We are like pipes that carry glory to a God who is capable of holding it. When humans are saddled with glory, we see stress, anxiety, depression, substance abuse, and even suicide; we just aren't meant to hold the glory in our lives that is meant for God.

I chose Exodus 15:2 for this day because I think this reflects a humble Eight's heart quite well. God is your strength; praise and glory be to Him. God is your salvation; praise and glory be to Him. And your life is about exulting Him. Amen.

SHIFT IN FOCUS

Memorize Exodus 15:2.

Paul tells us in 1 Corinthians 10:31, *"So, whether you eat or drink, or whatever you do, do all to the glory of God."*

How do you live this out? Where in your life are you tempted to hoard the glory meant for God?

10 DAYS OF LUST
How the Enemy Wants You to Stop Reflecting God

● ● ● ● ● ● ● ● ● ● ● **DAY 11**

What Is a Deadly Sin?

> *If anyone is caught in any transgression, you who are spiritual*
> *should restore him in a spirit of gentleness. Keep watch on yourself,*
> *lest you too be tempted.* (Galatians 6:1)

Although the wording or specific idea for the "seven deadly sins"
is not in the Bible, the list of them has been used by Christians
for ages. The classification of seven deadly sins that we know
today was first penned by a monk named Evagrius Ponticus who
lived from AD 345–399.

This list has gone through many changes since its origi-
nation, but it has remained a helpful way for us to name the
common vices that keep us in chains.

When these seven sins are paired with specific Enneagram
numbers (plus two extra sins to make nine), they give us a better

idea of the specific vices that may be tripping us up again and again. This is important because these problems are often blind spots in our lives. Their exposure leads us to repentance, better health, and greater unity with Christ, which is the greatest thing learning about our Enneagram number can do for us.

Here are the deadly sins early Enneagram teachers paired with each type:

1. Anger
2. Pride
3. Deceit
4. Envy
5. Greed
6. Fear
7. Gluttony
8. Lust
9. Sloth

Struggling with one of these sins dominantly does not mean that you do not struggle with all of them. If we are honest with ourselves and humble, we can all recognize ourselves in each of the sins listed. However, your dominant deadly sin is a specific tool Satan will use to distract the world from seeing how you reflect God.

For Eights, the deadly sin you struggle with most is lust, but not exclusively of a sexual nature. Whether or not you recognize lust in your own life as you're thinking about it now, I entreat you to give great thought to it in these next ten days.

Exposing blind spots in our life can feel a lot like ripping off a bandage that we might prefer to leave on, but what's underneath is God-honoring and beautiful.

SHIFT IN FOCUS

Spend some time contemplating and praying about what lust might look like in your life.

What does that word actually mean when you look it up?

Does it surprise you to see that specific sin printed next to your Enneagram number?

DAY 12 • • • • • • • • • • • •

What Is Lust?

Beloved, I urge you as sojourners and exiles to abstain from the
passions of the flesh, which wage war against your soul.
(1 Peter 2:11)

The dictionary defines lust as a passionate or overmastering desire or craving. Of course, it can describe a sexual desire, but when we are talking about Eights' deadly sin, we are usually talking about any overwhelming desire, not merely a sexual one.

We tend to hear *lust* used in only the sexual sense because our culture is obsessed with sex. We saw this vividly in the 1990s with the wave of purity culture, and every Bible verse that *could* be talking about sex was translated or twisted to mean so. Sexual sin is considered one of the *big* sins in many of our churches today, which is why so many of us hide our sexual sin or don't come forward when we've been sinned against sexually. For many Christians, there is a lot of shame in this area, and that shame can keep people stuck even though God wants them to be free.

I can see this being a big part of Satan's plan: "Distract them with *big sins*, and they'll fail to recognize the *little* sins I'm slowly drowning them in."

We see in the Bible that there are no little or big sins. One translation of Matthew 5:21–22 reads like this:

You have heard that our ancestors were told, "You must not
murder. If you commit murder, you are subject to judgment."

*But I say, if you are even angry with someone, you are sub-
ject to judgment! If you call someone an idiot, you are in
danger of being brought before the court. And if you curse
someone, you are in danger of the fires of hell.* (NLT)

God is so holy, and His standard for righteousness is so high,
that you are accountable for even muttering "you idiot" under
your breath at someone, even if they really *are* dumb. This is still
sinning, and it's sin that Jesus had to die for.

So when we think about lust, we have to do a little repro-
gramming. The lust we are talking about is not the *big sin* lust,
but sin in disguise. What we are trying to pinpoint for you, dear
Eight, is something entirely different than sexual lust.

Lust can look like intense energy, an overpowering desire, or
a forceful pull toward anything that is not yours to have or yours
to do.

Lust is an emotional, mental, and physical desire, which is
why it is so powerful. First Peter 2:11 tells us, *"The passions of the
flesh...wage war against your soul."*

Lust is a hook, and once you've been caught, it's almost
impossible to break free. This is because the desires of our flesh
are strong, going down to our core instincts, and we, as humans,
are weak against its cravings.

SHIFT IN FOCUS

What is the first verse you think of when you hear the word
lust?

Have you ever heard of lust in any context other than sexual desire?

Can you see the description of lust that we discussed as something that you struggle with in your life?

• • • • • • • • • • • DAY 13

What Lust Means for Eights

So flee youthful passions and pursue righteousness, faith, love, and
peace, along with those who call on the Lord from a pure heart.
(2 Timothy 2:22)

If lust means having an intense desire or need for something, why is that a sin? Well, having a strong desire or drive isn't bad, but whether it's moral depends on the object of your desire. So, today, I want to propose that lust gets in the way of how Eights reflect God by disguising itself as intense energy—but it's an energy that often leads Eights toward something that is not theirs or not theirs to do.

Lust is impulsive. It's about immediate gratification and the surge of energy that comes from the pursuit. But sometimes you were never asked to join the pursuit, you aren't ready to pursue this, and there doesn't even need to be a pursuit!

You may have heard that Eights punch first and ask questions later. This is what we are talking about when we speak of lust. You may feel justified in the action you're taking only to realize later that you didn't have the full story, or didn't take the time to weigh your actions against the consequences.

In my coaching practice, one of the questions I ask potential Eights is, "Did you ever punch someone when you were a child?" It's still amazing to me that every Eight I've interviewed has said yes or has come back to me later and said, "I guess I didn't remember this story, but my sibling did, and…" For a lot of Eights, this type of impulsive behavior, protection, and action is so embedded into your instincts that it's not a childhood memory that even sticks out. It wasn't weird or odd that you punched someone; it felt justified—perhaps it even felt like the only option!

For Eights, this happens because of the perfect storm of being in the gut triad, having a strong protective instinct, and having abundant energy and confidence. I've heard Eights say, "My gut has never steered me wrong." But is that 100 percent true? If you trust your own gut more than you trust what God says in His word about pursuing *"righteousness, faith, love, and peace,"* you will make impulsive decisions that are being driven by lust—and are the wrong decisions.

SHIFT IN FOCUS

A lot of this problem area for Eights gets ironed out in their teen years and early twenties, when it gets them into the most trouble. But it's still something to be abundantly aware of even if you're older and no longer as aware of the lust in your life.

Do you act first?

Do you forget to question your gut?

Do you pursue righteousness, faith, love, and peace?

• • • • • • • • • • • **DAY 14**

Calling Lust What It Is

But put on the Lord Jesus Christ, and make no provision for the flesh, to gratify its desires. (Romans 13:14)

Calling impulsiveness and intensity "lust" can be a really hard pill to swallow. Part of this is because you've felt "too much" for others, and a natural coping mechanism to this hurt is to fully embrace and become proud of your "too much-ness." In and of itself, this is fine. I want you to fully embrace and be proud of who God made you to be and your unique strengths. However, this pride can get in the way of seeing lust for what it really is in your life.

Eights' defense mechanism is denial. If there is something too big in your life that you don't think you can change, you might deny it even exists. As an Eight, it is good to be aware of this tendency and ask yourself about it often. This coping mechanism might even be tricking you into believing that *nothing* is too big and unchangeable in your life.

Lust is one of the areas in an Eight's life that they tend to be either proud of or deny the existence of. This is why it's so important for you to recognize the lust in your life and to call lust what it is: a sin.

When you act on impulse without all the information, there is a great likelihood that you are sinning. Maybe the action itself is not sinful, but did you, for example, sin against your brother by taking action too quickly? Did you leave someone feeling unheard or inept?

When you pursue something with all your energy, you might be leaving people behind or, worse, deflecting wise counsel. God's Word tells us, *"Desire without knowledge is not good, and whoever makes haste with his feet misses his way"* (Proverbs 19:2).

Do you react with anger and use your full strength to intimidate? This is sin.

Is the object of your intense desire something that isn't yours or isn't supposed to be yours yet? Then acting on or dwelling in that intense desire is sin.

Do you pursue fights and battles that are not your responsibility, therefore taking away the chance for the responsible party to obediently engage in their own battle? This is sin.

God's standards for us are much higher than we like to think they are. We like to think that there is some way we can live completely pleasing to God in our own power and with all of our excuses. But we are sinful, and there is no shame in admitting that, only humility.

SHIFT IN FOCUS

Where in your life do you need to name lust?

Spend some time in prayer and reflection, asking God to examine your heart and reveal your ways that are displeasing to Him.

• • • • • • • • • • • **DAY 15**

Why Satan Wants Your Energy

For this is the will of God, your sanctification: that you abstain from
sexual immorality; that each one of you know how to control his
own body in holiness and honor, not in the passion of lust like the
Gentiles who do not know God. (1 Thessalonians 4:3–5)

The enemy wants you to believe your energy and full-steam-ahead, lustful drive are good, no matter what. If he can keep you charging toward the wrong thing, or things that are simply not yours to do, he has captured your energy and controls you—even while you still think you're in control.

The enemy would love you to call your lust "high energy," "passion," "knowing what you want," or even "impulsiveness," but it's important to identify and call it what it is.

Eights reflect God's strength, justice, zeal, vigilance, and tenderness. As an Eight, you are such an amazing reflection of God the Father and how He boldly and strongly loves us. However, lust leads others to distrust Eights. People might not tell an Eight everything that's going on in their life because it risks igniting energy that could lead to reckless action. Lust can lead others to resent Eights and dismiss their justice, protection, and zeal because they've "mowed them over" in the past.

This not only distracts from the ways you reflect God, but sometimes your lust is so loud that all of the good you're actually doing can no longer be heard, much less be an opportunity to bring glory to God.

There have been Eights in my life whom I've refused to go to when I've been victimized out of fear that their action in trying to protect me might bring them to ruin. This means they cannot use their protective nature and giftings in that area safely while exercising self-control, which is so sad. The lust in their life has overshadowed how beautifully they reflect God.

This is all a part of you having responsibility for your strength. The way in which you reflect God is not a quiet reflection. You get to be on the front lines; you are a soldier God has entrusted with great responsibility. And if Satan can't have your eternity, he will steal your testimony and effectiveness with lust.

SHIFT IN FOCUS

These days on lust are hard and blunt, but I know you can handle it.

I trust that you can take these words to God and examine their truthfulness in your life for yourself. Some of these words might not be true for you, and I praise God for that, but humility openly looks at the facts and thoughtfully weighs them against reality.

Take some time today to reflect on how lust might be sneaking into your life.

Ask someone if they trust you to have wisdom and self-control when it comes to protecting those you love.

• • • • • • • • • • • • DAY 16

The Temptation of Reckless Action
By Carolyn Clare Givens

But each person is tempted when he is lured and enticed by his own desire. Then desire when it has conceived gives birth to sin, and sin when it is fully grown brings forth death. (James 1:14–15)

Envision this scenario: you come out of a meeting absolutely certain that the next thing to do is call up your boss and make sure *he* knows what *you* know. You know exactly how everything he just talked about should be implemented in the company and what the pitfalls are going to be. You *know* that he can't be aware of all the information and group dynamics you see playing out every day. Your voice should be heard here—you've got something valuable to contribute.

Let's take this hypothetical case to the next level. You get a private meeting with your boss. You tell him everything you want to say. You give him advice on how to move forward and the issues he's going to face. You might even point out a few problem people whom you already know will gum up the works and impede progress and efficiency. You can see the direction his vision leads, and you know the path of least resistance to get there.

And when you are done speaking, your boss says, "I'm sorry, I think you misunderstood. The board has a different direction for us."

At best, you're embarrassed. At worst—well, there are many potential outcomes.

It sometimes feels like we Eights can see the future. We're tracking the power dynamics of the situation. We're gaming out the rest of the story and we *know*—I mean, *know*—deep in our bones *exactly* how it's all going to turn out. And if everyone would just *listen* to us, we'd be able to fix it all. We'd make it work out, just by sheer force of will.

But there's always the chance that we *don't* know the whole story. We *can't* actually see the future. Our desire to make everything work out the way we think it's supposed to is rooted in pride, in control, and, ultimately, in sin. When we lean into that without hesitation—as it is so easy to do—we may wreak consequences and damage we cannot even imagine in the moment. For as James tells us, desire leads to sin, and sin ultimately leads to death.

SHIFT IN FOCUS

Have you ever acted recklessly or thoughtlessly and seen the damage that came from that decision?

Have you ever hurt someone because of your tendency to jump in and take control of a situation?

Reflect on today's Scripture passage and devotional. Is God calling you to repent of sin?

• • • • • • • • • • • • DAY 17

What Is Godly Action?
By Carolyn Clare Givens

And whatever you do, in word or deed, do everything in the name
of the Lord Jesus, giving thanks to God the Father through him.
(Colossians 3:17)

Everything. Words, actions—*whatever.*

Do *everything* in the name of the Lord Jesus, giving thanks to the Father through Him.

How does that even work?

For Eights, this little command in Colossians requires a daily—or perhaps hourly...or perhaps minute-by-minute—handing over of the reins of our lives to Jesus. It's a regular, conscious decision that we are not the ones in control of this thing called life. And it's a regular, conscious choice to evaluate our motivations for our actions. Are we doing this in the name of the Lord Jesus? Are we doing this for the good of others?

Godly action is thoughtful. It considers the hearts of the people around us and whether our words and deeds would be beneficial to them.

Godly action is tempered. It doesn't enter the situation with guns blazing, asking questions later. It considers the context of the moment and takes into account all of the factors.

As Eights, when we're taking action, our intent is usually to be helpful and positive. We're not typically trying to burn down the world around us. We want to protect. But we have to pair that goal with an intention to do good *in the way* we work, not just the end result. For what does it profit anyone if we get the result we wanted, but we damaged relationships along the way?

It isn't always easy to take a moment (or a few days) to pray and consider a situation before acting. It isn't easy to admit that our approach may not be the best option out there. It isn't easy to hand over the reins to Jesus in every moment, in every action.

But He is trustworthy, so we don't have to fear. He will care for and protect those around us better than we can. He will work His will more powerfully than we could.

And He will guide us so that we are *"equipped for every good work"* (2 Timothy 3:17), even those we didn't see coming.

SHIFT IN FOCUS

Are you doing everything in the name of the Lord Jesus Christ? What reminders can you spread throughout your day to point you back to the regular, conscious choice to let Him be in charge?

Memorize Colossians 3:17 and recall it to your mind throughout the days ahead, especially when you're making decisions that will affect the people around you.

• • • • • • • • • • • **DAY 18**

The Ten-Second Rule

With all humility and gentleness, with patience, bearing with one another in love. (Ephesians 4:2)

Dear Eight, your strength and gusto for life are so admirable. As you process and think about the topic of lust and what it means to recognize this in your life, reflect on what is yours to do and how you can prioritize those things.

What are your three main responsibilities in life?

1. _____

2. _____

3. _____

How often do you see a need and just do it? Being an Eight means that you value things being done well and take a lot of responsibility for every area in your life. However, it could make all the difference if you saw a need and gave yourself ten seconds to think of someone else who could do it before claiming it as your responsibility. If it doesn't involve one of those three responsibilities you just listed, then it doesn't *need* to be yours to do.

I know it can be hard not to take on the world when it seems like you're the only person willing to do it, but practicing self-control and waiting even ten more seconds for someone else to volunteer in a group chat or board meeting can free you up to do what you're actually passionate about.

It may feel silly, and ten seconds will feel like a lifetime in the moment. But chances are you have ten seconds to spare. And those ten seconds could be the difference between burnout and saving your sanity.

There are so many times someone might be ready to volunteer but don't get the chance because you've jumped in to take on the job. Most people wait before raising their hand; they might need more information about what's involved or want to ask questions. But as an Eight, you probably have already decided. Others might also know you'll take something on if there is any amount of awkward silence, so they'll wait for you to take the task before even processing if it's something they could or should do. Ten seconds gives others time to recognize that you will give others a chance and enable them to evaluate whether they actually can do the task.

Being quick to act is something you share with Enneagram Threes (the Achiever) and Sevens (the Enthusiast), so you might know how this feels on the receiving end as well. God will let you know when it's time for you to act. *"Be still before the LORD and wait patiently for him"* (Psalm 37:7).

SHIFT IN FOCUS

What's something you have on your plate right now that you could delegate to another?

Do you want to shift out of one of the responsibilities on your list?

How can you better focus on your three main responsibilities?

● ● ● ● ● ● ● ● ● ● ● ● **DAY 19**

Finding Your Brakes
By Carolyn Clare Givens

"Be still, and know that I am God. I will be exalted among the nations, I will be exalted in the earth!" (Psalm 46:10)

Have you ever been brought to a standstill by your strength crashing down around you? Maybe you were being productive and efficient and then you got sick and couldn't do anything except lie in bed. Or maybe you were keeping up with regular time with the Lord and prayer until a tragedy struck and you suddenly found God unapproachable.

We Eights have a tendency to push and push and push ourselves until we physically, mentally, spiritually, or emotionally break down. We go from highly effective and efficient to *nothing*: sixty to zero instead of the other way around.

One of the ways to mitigate the crashes is to find ways to regularly pump our brakes and step away from the go-go-go of our lives to pause, reflect, and consider the big picture. When we are still, we can reorient ourselves and our place in relationship to God. We can be still and know that He is God and He will be exalted.

For each one of us, this practice will be different. Here are some ideas you could consider:

+ Schedule regular coffee dates with a trusted friend who will ask you hard questions and help you to reflect and evaluate yourself physically, mentally, spiritually, and emotionally.

+ Take a walk each week with your phone zipped away in a pocket and breathe deeply of God's creation.

+ Find a passage of Scripture that inspires you and spend time with it each day until you have it memorized. Consider starting with Psalm 121.

+ Take up a Scripture engagement practice, such as handwriting Scripture, reading it aloud, or drawing a picture in response to it—anything that slows you down and physically engages you with your text for that day.

+ Take up a "focal practice." This is a phrase used by philosopher Albert Borgmann to refer to an activity that makes life meaningful, such as reciting poetry, playing a musical instrument, painting, rock collecting, gardening, and the like.

SHIFT IN FOCUS

How often do you find your brakes? Is it a regular practice in your life?

If it is, pause and thank God for the benefits you see from this practice. Does this practice help you to be still and know that God is God? Evaluate how it's going and see if you want to change what you do or add any new practices.

If it is not, find an activity—perhaps from the list in today's devotional or something else you think will ground you—that will help you to be still and begin implementing it on a weekly or monthly basis.

DAY 20 • • • • • • • • • • •

Living Under God's Authority

Everyone who goes on ahead and does not abide in the teaching of Christ, does not have God. Whoever abides in the teaching has both the Father and the Son. (2 John 1:9)

Living under authority might not come naturally to you as an Eight. You've learned to trust yourself, but you distrust most other people, having known those who are fickle, incompetent, or selfish.

The idea of someone else deciding what you should do and how you should do it can prompt a visceral reaction from you. *How about no!*

You're most comfortable being by yourself, responsible for only you, or leading the pack—and there's not much in between.

The good news is that living under God's authority is very different from living under human authority. The latter simply cannot be pure, selfless, and righteous. But God can *only* be pure, holy, righteous, and good.

God gives us rules not because He delights in controlling us, but because, like a good Father, His intention is our good. He sets up boundaries and tells us not to cross them because He knows the consequences of us going off on our own. He wants us to prosper under His rules and live knowing we will never be betrayed by Him. He fully sees us and loves us.

God is not man, that he should lie, or a son of man, that he should change his mind. Has he said, and will he not do it? Or has he spoken, and will he not fulfill it? (Numbers 23:19)

If you've experienced trauma and tragedy, it can be hard to think of God as good, but that's okay. As theologian Paul Tillich said, "Doubt is not the opposite of faith; it is an element of faith."[2] You can have doubts and questions. God is big enough to walk with you through them. He's not bothered by your questions, your anger at Him, or your thoughts. But He does ask that if we profess to love Him, we walk in obedience.

If you love me, you will keep my commandments. (John 14:15)

Why do you call me "Lord, Lord," and not do what I tell you? (Luke 6:46)

Walking in obedience is just another way of saying "living under the authority of Christ." God must be the absolute authority over your life, or lust is just waiting to take you for a ride.

SHIFT IN FOCUS

If you would like to read about what obedience to God looks like, the book of James offers lots of practical examples.

The truth is, all of us are living under the authority of something, whether it's God, ourselves, or sin.

---

2. Paul Tillich, *Systematic Theology, Volume Two, Existence and the Christ* (Chicago: University of Chicago Press, 1958), 116.

Do you struggle to accept God's authority in your life, or is this an area that has become easier for you?

10 DAYS OF TENDERNESS
Your Strength and How to Use It

• • • • • • • • • • • **DAY 21**

What Is Tenderness?

He will tend his flock like a shepherd; he will gather the lambs in his arms; he will carry them in his bosom, and gently lead those that are with young. (Isaiah 40:11)

We use the word *tender* or *tenderness* in a couple of different ways:

+ As an adjective, *tender* means an object that is soft, sore, or easily broken. You can have a tender bruise, a tender piece of steak, or a tender plant that cannot survive either extreme hot or cold temperatures.

+ As a noun where we are talking about the name of something, like chicken tenders.

+ As a verb, *tender* may describe someone's heart or disposition toward something. This is where we get the concept of being tenderhearted. Being tender means to soften yourself toward a person, animal, situation, or object, usually because you know the thing you're facing is weak, young, scared, small, or simply just not as strong as you are.

For the next nine days, we are going to be talking about tender as a verb. This type of tenderness is a strength of type Eights that is mentioned infrequently.

Contrary to popular belief, tenderheartedness is something Eights access naturally. I see many Eights frustrated with how they are portrayed in culture and social media. When other types get a Disney princess to represent their type, Eights always get the villain. When other types are represented by Rudolf the Red-Nosed Reindeer, Eights are the Grinch. You're seen as cold or distant, and, in some cases, mean and hardhearted. Dear Eight, I know this is frustrating, and as a representative of Enneagram culture myself, I'm very sorry for this inaccurate portrayal.

I hope the coming days help you feel a little more understood and encourage your heart in this strength of yours.

SHIFT IN FOCUS

Is there a person, situation, or animal in your life with whom or with which you try to be tender?

Take a moment and pray for God to continue to show you opportunities for your tenderness to grow and bless others. If these words reflect your heart, please borrow them:

Dear heavenly Father, we are so blessed by Your tenderness with us. I pray that You would continue to grow this gift in me and convict me of the areas where I need to be tenderhearted and am not. Give me eyes to see the people who need my tenderness. Amen.

DAY 22 • • • • • • • • • • •

How Are Eights Tender?

Be kind to one another, tenderhearted, forgiving one another, as God in Christ forgave you. (Ephesians 4:32)

Your tenderness will play an important role in who you are as an Eight. Many of the Eights I know revolve their entire lives around the areas that bring out the most tenderness in them. They are foster parents, pastors, nurses, caretakers for the elderly, and teachers. I think this is because the people who you feel the most tenderness toward give you the biggest sense of purpose. After all, who is a guardian without someone to guard? Or a soldier without something to fight for?

As an Eight, you wear thick armor, and that's what most people see: hard, strong, in control. But this armor is only necessary because underneath it is the softest heart. This is a heart that you save for those who need it most. I've heard an Eight say, "I need to save my softness for my kids because I don't have much to give, and I can't waste it here."

I've seen the strongest people be the most considerate and loving with children or animals. Sometimes the people others are scared of feel like the safest people to me. I've seen Eights' armor melt away when they're dealing with someone hurting.

Eights have this ability to sense when someone is weaker than they are, and they are purposefully careful with them, as if they are dealing with someone's wound. Usually the weakness they sense is an obvious one; for instance, perhaps the person is a child or elderly. Yet sometimes, Eights can sense more subtle weaknesses, like mental weariness, immaturity, the lack of a vital relationship, or the need for guidance.

SHIFT IN FOCUS

Who or what in your life receives your tenderness?

In today's verse from Ephesians, tenderness is bookended by two other commands: being kind and forgiving. Do you find those two commands to be challenging?

DAY 23 • • • • • • • • • • •

How Your Tenderness Reflects God

When he saw the crowds, he had compassion for them, because they were harassed and helpless, like sheep without a shepherd. (Matthew 9:36)

In the Bible, we see over and over again the correlation between God being our shepherd and us being His sheep. One reason for this repetition is that this relationship reflects the tenderness God feels toward us. He is gentle and careful with the areas of our hearts that are easily broken.

Like sheep, we are also fickle, foolish, and prone to wander. In Matthew 9:36, we see an example of Jesus's tender heart toward the people He encountered daily. He had compassion for the crowds of people who were listening to His words and seeking healing because He saw their need, their weakness, and how greatly they needed a Savior. He viewed them as sheep without a shepherd because that's how we are without our life tethered to God through Christ.

You reflect the tenderness of God when you are tender toward the people in your life. In this way, you get to be the hands and feet of our tender God for those who are helpless, lost, and broken.

Eights are built to hold with tenderness the people who need it the most. You have an energy that few can match, your protective instincts are sharp, and your tenderness is an unexpected but much-needed surprise to many.

Whether it's with a child, an animal, someone who is lost, or someone who is about to take their last breath, you reflect God's tenderness to His people and the special place in His heart for the hurting.

SHIFT IN FOCUS

In what area of your life is your tenderness on display the most?

Spend some time thanking God for the honor of reflecting His tenderness, and ask Him to help you give the glory of your tenderness to Him.

DAY 24 • • • • • • • • • • •

Strong and Tender: How They Work Together
By Carolyn Clare Givens

At that very hour some Pharisees came and said to him, "Get away from here, for Herod wants to kill you." And he said to them, "Go and tell that fox, 'Behold, I cast out demons and perform cures today and tomorrow, and the third day I finish my course. Nevertheless, I must go on my way today and tomorrow and the day following, for it cannot be that a prophet should perish away from Jerusalem.' O Jerusalem, Jerusalem, the city that kills the prophets and stones those who are sent to it! How often would I have gathered your children together as a hen gathers her brood under her wings, and you were not willing!"
(Luke 13:31–34)

Dear Challenger, you're not alone when you lament. Jesus saw the abuses of power around Him and knew that He Himself was the way of salvation for those being abused. He saw they were blind, and He lamented over Jerusalem.

The image in this passage in Luke (and its parallel in Matthew 23) is one of the most powerful to me of all of Jesus's words. He cries out to Jerusalem in judgment and sorrow. He calls Herod a fox, and He sets His face like flint toward His purpose—the sacrifice on the cross—never flinching once at what He knows is to come. And then He uses the picture of a hen gathering her chicks under her wings to protect them.

I once heard a story of a barnyard fire that had decimated a farm. As the farmer walked through the wreckage, he saw the blackened feathers of one of his chickens, lost in the heat and flame, her wings outstretched. Taking a stick, he lifted the dead bird and discovered there, protected from death, her chicks, alive and huddled together. She had sacrificed herself for them.

I think of that story every time I hear Jesus's lament over Jerusalem. He was strong enough to sacrifice Himself on behalf of the whole world, and He was tender enough to care about the ones who had rejected His protection.

Oh, no, we are not alone when we lament.

SHIFT IN FOCUS

Who needs your strength today? And how is your tenderness going to serve those same individuals? Where can you bring these two gifts together?

DAY 25 • • • • • • • • • • • •

The Tender Coworker

A new commandment I give to you, that you love one another:
just as I have loved you, you also are to love one another.
By this all people will know that you are my disciples,
if you have love for one another.
(John 13:34–35)

The workplace is a complicated place and looks different for each of us. Whether you're a boss or a new hire, chances are you work alongside other people. These coworkers are people you often don't choose, but they heavily impact your day-to-day life, for better or worse.

Eights are a great asset to the workplace when it comes to getting things done and moving forward. But that strength brings the problem of you steaming ahead and running over people in the process. I know what you're thinking: *If I sat around all day and was careful with everyone's feelings, we would never get any work done!* That's not what I'm telling you to do.

Danielle, who you read about in the chapter entitled "What It Means to Be a Challenger," told me this:

> I was talking about this with my sister Kayla, and she said this: "Danielle, Eights put the pedal to the metal in everything they do! They're full-force ahead up the mountain. Nobody else can keep up with that and, often, most are too scared to even try! But if you learned

that you could make it up that mountain with your pedal still gaining some good speed, still with your passion and enthusiasm, just not down to the floor, engines revving, then that would give people a chance to keep up with you—or at least not scare them so much." This has been so helpful in all of my relationships! Being me, but also being sensitive to the fact that others don't react and move and dream and go like I do. And I can be sensitive to that.

Being sensitive to others' lack doesn't mean you need to change who you are; it just means that it's kind to notice others' limitations and slow down a little. This moment of noticing and slowing down will help your coworkers feel loved, seen, and supported. At the end of the day, that will contribute to a better workday for everyone, which often correlates to more work being done.

You don't need to be everyone's best friend or cater to weakness...but the Bible does charge you to be loving. *"By this all people will know that you are my disciples, if you have love for one another."*

SHIFT IN FOCUS

What does being conscious of not "steaming ahead" look like for you?

What does loving your coworkers look like this week?

Choose one action step and commit to doing it this week. This could even be asking some of your coworkers for feedback on how you could better serve them at work.

DAY 26 • • • • • • • • • • •

The Tender Leader

You have given me the shield of your salvation, and your right hand supported me, and your gentleness made me great.
(Psalm 18:35)

Where in your life are you a leader? This might be an easy question for you to answer, or perhaps you'll need to dig in order to find the answer. We are leaders in our lives as parents, older siblings, or even as friends. And of course, sometimes we are leaders in more traditional ways, like in a work environment.

Depending on your level of health, being tender as a leader might come easily to you, or it may not. Think of the people you lead right now. What's happening inside you when you picture them? Does your heart swell with protective energy, or do your lips purse in frustration? The people you're leading can tell whether that feeling in you is positive or negative. If anything is true of Eights, it's that others can feel tenderness or hardness from them. You might imagine your hardness just feels like apathy, but to many, it feels like anger, especially to those in the heart triad—Twos, Threes, and Fours—who are very socially attuned. This is one of the reasons people think Eights are intimidating.

If you are a leader, one of the greatest pieces of advice I can give you comes from Psalm 18:35: *"Your gentleness made me great."* Tough love is not the only option when it comes to motivating someone, but since that is going to be your default, focusing on gentleness will help you find the balance between showing gentleness and toughness toward those you lead.

What does gentleness as a leader look like?

+ Praising what's praiseworthy

+ Cooling off before correcting

+ Asking for feedback

+ Communicating clearly (and using some proverbial hand-holding)

+ Not venting about those you lead in the building where you work

+ Prioritizing your relationship with God above everything

SHIFT IN FOCUS

I learned about *totems* from Suzanne Stabile. A totem is something that will remind you of what you're working on or trying to grow in. They can be as extreme as a tattoo of a Bible verse, or as simple as a sticky note on your mirror.

This week, I'd like you to make a totem out of that list of what gentleness as a leader looks like, or Psalm 18:35, whichever is more meaningful for you to read.

DAY 27 • • • • • • • • • • •

The Tender Friend
By Carolyn Clare Givens

But a Samaritan, as he journeyed, came to where he was, and when
he saw him, he had compassion. He went to him and bound up
his wounds, pouring on oil and wine. Then he set him on his own
animal and brought him to an inn and took care of him.
(Luke 10:33–34)

The parable of the good Samaritan is one of the most familiar in
Scripture. We hear it taught over and over, and the story's expan-
sion of Jesus's command to love *"your neighbor as yourself"* (Luke
10:27) helps us to understand our calling as obedient children
of God.

On the one hand, we Eights can find it difficult to follow this
commandment. Loving our neighbor as ourselves means that we
have to let down our walls a bit. We might even need to let someone else into our inner circle. But on the other hand, this is the
most natural and simple command to follow; we are being asked
to protect someone weaker than ourselves.

One of the names for the Enneagram Eight is the Protector.
Standing up and being the shield against the world is no problem at all. But the flip side of this is where we really shine: while
we shield, we also care. We wrap our arms (figuratively or literally) around our friend or neighbor and we tend to their wounds.

We hold them in our strength, fending off everything coming at them, and we soothe their pain. They are safe.

"You are safe" is one of the most powerful phrases we have. In his *hierarchy of needs*, psychologist Abraham Maslow (1908–1970) listed the most basic needs as first physiological—food, water, warmth, and rest—and then safety, including security.[3] Until these two sets of needs are met, we struggle to even think about proceeding on toward emotional and spiritual needs. An Eight's tender strength is a boon here. We can stand between our friend and the harsh world, and pour out the oil and wine of our care over them.

SHIFT IN FOCUS

Who is your neighbor? Who needs you to pour your care into them today? Have you taken time to ask this question recently? If you have not, please say this prayer with me:

> Dear heavenly Father, open my eyes today to the physical, emotional, and spiritual needs of those around me. Help me to see where I can make a safe space for someone who is hurting. Give me the courage to open my circle to that friend and the fortitude to use my shield for their care, instead of just for my own. Give me the wisdom to see their needs and how I can tenderly serve and care for them. Amen.

---

3. Dr. Saul McLeod, "Maslow's Hierarchy of Needs," *Simply Psychology*, updated December 29, 2020, www.simplypsychology.org/maslow.html.

DAY 28 • • • • • • • • • • •

The Tender Parent
By Dave Harris

Children, obey your parents in the Lord, for this is right. "Honor
your father and mother" (this is the first commandment with a
promise), "that it may go well with you and that you may live long in
the land." Fathers, do not provoke your children to anger, but bring
them up in the discipline and instruction of the Lord.
(Ephesians 6:1–4)

A verse with a commandment for our children to show us
honor can lead us, as parents and Eights, to have feelings of righteous indignation if a child fails to follow this commandment.
After all, don't these children want to have it go well with them?
Do they not want to live long in the land? Wouldn't it be much
easier for us as parents if they would just do what is right?

We want to challenge, correct, and change our children's
course because we are convinced we see the right way! But then
we, as parents, are hit with a stark reminder that we must be careful to not *"provoke [our] children to anger."* The Scripture doesn't
just stop there. We are also instructed to *"bring them up in the dis-*
cipline and instruction of the Lord." These verses are just as much
of a command for us as parents as they are to our children.

The Lord is a perfect Father: tender, loving, compassionate,
and just. Scripture is packed with reminders of God examining

the motives of man, not just mere behavior. This is what we're called to emulate as parents when it comes to bringing up our children in all aspects of their lives—discipline included.

Whether you find this easy or difficult, the Spirit living inside of you can help you in these moments. Depending on your health, your first reaction to your child in a situation where correction is needed may not be the appropriate one. You must learn to hear from the Holy Spirit so that you are not immediately reacting, or you may provoke your child to anger. To be clear, a child may still be angry with discipline, but we as parents must ensure that our motives, in whatever consequences take place, are those that seek to honor the Lord and point our child toward Him, rather than motives to make our lives easier or make us feel vindicated.

When you do provoke your children to anger, one of the most fruitful ways to rectify that situation is with a sincere and heartfelt apology followed by asking for their forgiveness. In modeling repentance, we are modeling a relationship of trust and reconciliation. We are demonstrating that grace is available to us all as God's children when we fall short; we are modeling the good news of the gospel!

Your tenderness can and should be shown to your kids through your obedience to God and His Word. (See Deuteronomy 6:6–7.) Show love and care for them by caring about their lives and any issues they are going through. Ask questions that clarify motives and feelings rather than assuming you know how they are feeling because of their actions. They will feel most safe and most loved when you respond with understanding, care, and concern.

SHIFT IN FOCUS

Do you want to be tenderer in your relationship with your kids? Pray with me:

Dear heavenly Father, please continue to lead me in Your ways when it comes to raising the children You have given me. I admit that I do not always do things in a way that will not provoke anger. Please convict me when I am tempted to discipline in anger and with wrong motives. Father, I do not understand all the feelings that my kids have, but I truly want to. Thank You for seeing me as Your child. Thank You for examining my heart and motives with a loving and just Father's heart. Please help me to see with Your eyes, hear with Your ears, and respond in Your ways. Amen.

• • • • • • • • • • • **DAY 29**

The Tender Spouse
By Dave Harris

Wives, submit to your husbands, as is fitting in the Lord.
Husbands, love your wives, and do not be harsh with them.
(Colossians 3:18–19)

These loving words from the apostle Paul's letter to the church at Colossae represent many passages in Scripture that talk about the relationship between husbands and wives. They're a way to remind us that marriage is not easy, and it will take work, but it is worth it! Since marriage always involves two sinners, married life is bound to provide opportunities to live in repentance and grow as disciples of Jesus. In marriage, you as an Eight have a great opportunity to show the fierce love and care you have for your spouse, but you may also have a tendency to live in high intensity, be short-tempered, and become overbearing toward your loved one.

Eights can often be independent to a fault. You may feel that you have had to pick yourself up by your bootstraps, fend for yourself, and protect yourself. There is a high possibility that others have failed you…and will fail you again. You may feel that you need to push through life caring for the underdogs and being strong for others. You may feel that discussing your feelings on a matter is irrelevant to results, and therefore unnecessary. To a spouse, this can feel disrespectful, unloving, or harsh.

You were designed by God to be known by Him and others. You are not meant to go at it alone! If God has blessed you with a spouse, I guarantee that there are things happening in your life, mind, and soul that your spouse wants to know about.

Your spouse wants to know when you are feeling hurt or insecure. Your spouse will also find comfort in hearing that when you're struggling, you are choosing to trust in God more than you are choosing to rely on yourself.

Share your life. Open up to your spouse and let them speak into the things you are struggling with. I'll let you in on a secret: they already know that something is happening because none of us are that good at hiding it! No matter how much you try to mask your feelings, they show through in ways that you may not even be aware of. Opening up to talk about these things will help your spouse feel more connected to you, which will allow you to deepen your connection to each other while trusting that God is the way to find the solutions.

SHIFT IN FOCUS

What is a way in which you can trust that your spouse cares deeply for you?

Do you share the thoughts that keep you preoccupied with fear, doubt, worry, or concern?

In what way is God asking you to grow as a spouse this year? Pray for discernment in this today.

• • • • • • • • • • • DAY 30

The World Needs Your Tenderness
By Carolyn Clare Givens

Finally, all of you, have unity of mind, sympathy, brotherly love,
a tender heart, and a humble mind. Do not repay evil for evil or
reviling for reviling, but on the contrary, bless, for to this you were
called, that you may obtain a blessing. (1 Peter 3:8–9)

Dear Challenger, we live in a world that has learned to get high on outrage, the knee-jerk response we have when we're wronged—whether by our neighbor, our leaders, strangers, or our brothers and sisters in Christ. It's easy to let ourselves feel indignant and angry. It's not hard to get offended by someone or something.

But, oh, what a world we *could* live in. What if, instead of outrage, we responded with *"sympathy, brotherly love, a tender heart, and a humble mind"*? What if we did not *"repay evil for evil or reviling for reviling"*? What if we blessed those who cursed us?

Can you imagine it?

There are days when it seems like a lost cause. Even if I respond with blessing when reviling is pointed my way, that doesn't stop the reviling, does it? But here's the thing: we Eights could change the world if we wanted to. If we leaned into the grace of God and the strengths He gives us, we could influence our circles and grow them, and influence the circles we touch, and so on.

The world needs your tenderness, dear Eight. It needs an example of love in the face of outrage. It needs an example of blessing in the face of evil. It needs someone who can look forward and imagine a better way. And we are strong enough to do it.

Even as we grieve and lament the wrongness around us, we can stand for hope. Even as we fight the evil that comes against us, we can respond in blessing. Even as we come face to face with hardness, we can respond with tenderness. Even as we face outrage, we can respond with a humble mind.

We Eights are not alone in this. Others who know and love Jesus want these things, too. But so many times, even they need our tenderness to lead them. They need our strength to help them feel strong.

SHIFT IN FOCUS

If you resonate with these words, please pray with me:

Dear heavenly Father, when I look at everything going on in the world around me, my gut response is usually one of rage, but I know that You made me tender as well, and that You call me to give that gift to the world. Give me the strength to be tender, Lord. Give me patience and peace. Help me every day to return good for evil, blessing for rage. Help me to lead those around me to the same response, by your grace. Amen.

10 DAYS OF INTIMIDATION
Help with a Common Pain Point

Why Are Eights Seen as Intimidating?

We who are strong have an obligation to bear with the failings of the weak, and not to please ourselves. (Romans 15:1)

Have you ever been told you are intimidating? This is a common pain point for Eights as they traverse life and relationships. You can be the kindest person, quietest person, or the tiniest person in a room, and still be seen as intimidating. This is one of the most confusing things to the Eights I've talked to, as they don't view themselves as intimidating at all.

But then why is this true? Eights are the only Enneagram type with a commanding presence. Others can feel something from you that is hard to explain.

You have a lot of energy, you don't tiptoe around others' feelings, you have high standards, and you won't be controlled. All of these facts combine into a force that people can discern from you, and to be honest, it kind of scares them. They don't know what you'll do or say, but they know they may not have a good defense if you decide to go after them. They're in some way defenseless and helpless against you.

I know you don't often confront people, and if you do, there is a good reason. But that doesn't mean that people aren't still scared of your potential.

Others encounter you like they might a large dog. If someone has been attacked by a dog, or has even witnessed an attack, they know what a dog can do. Even if the dog they're encountering is the tamest, gentlest, calmest dog in the world, they're still going to be hesitant and careful around it—and understandably so. It's not the dog itself that they are scared of, but the potential they have as a species.

In a similar way, another Eight may have already ruined your reputation with many people you will encounter. People are hesitant and careful around you because they can recognize something that they saw in the person who harmed them. I know it may sound cliché and unhelpful, but try not to take their reaction personally.

It is hard to be a lion among sheep, even if you are a tame lion who is there to protect them.

SHIFT IN FOCUS
How has being seen as intimidating impacted your life?

Do you think being seen as intimidating has made you embrace it, or try really hard not to be seen this way?

DAY 32 • • • • • • • • • • •

But I'm Not Intimidating!

And the angel said to her, "Do not be afraid, Mary,
for you have found favor with God."
(Luke 1:30)

Being a lion in a lamb's world may be one of the most frustrating parts of being an Eight. You know how tender your heart is; your invisible armor is only there to protect you, not make it easier for you to launch a personal attack against anyone.

So it can be disheartening to hear over and over, "Are you angry?" or "When I first met you, I thought you were going to be mean," or "You intimidate me," or "Maybe you'd have more friends if you didn't come off this way."

It is hard to change something that you're not trying to do; it may not be possible for you to completely create an aura of meekness. No matter how gentle and tame you try to be, a lion is still a lion, and a lamb is still a lamb.

I find it interesting that in the Bible, every time an angel appears, people become frightened. It even goes so far as to say people are "in terror" at the sight of an angel, who must tell them, "Fear not!" Do angels do anything frightening? We don't exactly know; all Scripture tells us is that they showed up and God had very specific reasons for sending them, since angels are His messengers. If angels were less intimidating, perhaps people would not listen to them.

Instead of insisting "I'm not intimidating," you might be better served by accepting that, at least on the outside, you are just that. You might have to tell people that you're kind, gentle, and love being around them, even if you think you shouldn't have to. "I'm not as intimidating as I may come off at first, I promise!"

It's unfair that other Eights have made an impression on the people you meet before you've even had a chance, and that impacts how they see you. It's unfair that you have the softest heart, and people can't see that right away. It's unfair that you have to come with a qualifier while others are accepted as they are. But with the responsibility of being strong comes this pain point. You may have to show people how gentle you are.

SHIFT IN FOCUS

Read a couple of accounts of angels appearing to people in Scripture:

+ Genesis 21:17–19

+ Matthew 28:2–8

+ Luke 1:11–25

+ Luke 1:26–38

+ Luke 2:8–15

+ Acts 27:23–26

If you are weary or hurting because of how people have perceived you, take that weariness to God. He is strong and compassionate toward this area of hurt in your life. You don't need qualifiers or any explanation when it comes to God.

DAY 33 • • • • • • • • • •

Having a Presence

And he had a son whose name was Saul, a handsome young man.
There was not a man among the people of Israel more
handsome than he. From his shoulders upward
he was taller than any of the people.
(1 Samuel 9:2)

Having a presence means people notice you. This can be in an intimidating way, as we've already described, but it can also be in an awe-admiring way.

You may not literally stand head and shoulders above most people, as the Bible tells us King Saul did, but your presence makes people notice you all the same. Part of this noticing is motivated by attraction. Others are attracted to the way you carry yourself and seemingly don't care what the world has to say about you—although we know this may not be 100 percent true for you internally. This attraction leads people to follow you, even trust you.

This doesn't mean that people aren't also first intimidated by you. You may be confused to hear that a lot of people are attracted to your confidence because it doesn't feel like that; it feels like people are scared of you or push your buttons. But intimidation and attraction can often go hand and hand, and they do in this case.

As with strength, this magnetism comes with great responsibility. We see in the Bible that Saul ends up abusing his authority and power. His becoming fixated on keeping his power is what ultimately caused him to lose it. Being adored is addictive and often doesn't leave room for others to be adored.

I know you probably don't think that being overly admired is a problem in your life, but in one way or another, it is. So it's something to be aware of. There are people who are looking to you to see where to turn next and what they should do. Your voice is loud, and your presence speaks of leadership, whether you want it or not.

Many Eights in history (and in society today) abused the people who looked up to them, and I often get the impression that they had no idea what they were doing. "Why would they trust me that much?" "Why would they adore me? I'm pretty messed up. Can't they see that?"

You notice and respect people who are strong. Others feel the same way about you as an Eight. They want to follow, even if you don't want to lead.

SHIFT IN FOCUS

Are there people in your life who seem to be following you? Perhaps they hang on your every word, take your advice seriously, or often show up where you are.

If someone were to follow your example right now, would they be encouraged to become closer to Christ? Do they even know you're a Christian?

DAY 34 • • • • • • • • • • •

Is It Them and Not You?

Do not take to heart all the things that people say, lest you
hear your servant cursing you. Your heart knows that
many times you yourself have cursed others.
(Ecclesiastes 7:21–22)

Others being intimidated by you is ultimately not your responsibility. Some Eights do push into this image, but if you know you are truly not doing anything to make yourself appear to be aggressive and formidable, then being intimidating is not your identity. It means that others are easily intimidated, and that is not something you can control.

In Ecclesiastes, we see Solomon talk about not taking to heart what people say about you for a few reasons:

+ People are not your god. They don't get a say in your worth and identity.

+ People don't get a say in how God sees you.

+ We tend to take to heart the things people say about us.

+ Life is too short and people are too fickle for us to waste our time trying to conform.

This is wisdom. And although Scripture call us to pursue righteousness, love, and peace, it also clearly says, *"If possible, so far as it depends on you, live peaceably with all"* (Romans 12:18).

You do need to try, but not fixate. You do need to be courteous, but not change who God made you to be. How people react to you is not your responsibility, but theirs.

If you struggle with putting on the "intimidating" identity and leaning into it, I want to encourage you that this is not all of who you are. By embracing it, you are actually giving in to people's assumptions about you instead of challenging them.

SHIFT IN FOCUS

Is it hard for you not to take the way people see you to heart?

Do you struggle with leaning into your "intimidating" persona?

Spend a quiet moment with God and ask Him to search your heart for this lie: "I am who people say I am." Invite Him to embolden you with the truth: "I am who God says I am."

Write down three things God says you are versus three things people say you are. For example, "They say I'm intimidating, but God says I'm fearfully and wonderfully made."

+ They say_____,
  but God says _____.

+ They say_____,
  but God says_____.

+ They say_____,
  but God says _____.

DAY 35 • • • • • • • • • • • •

The Strong Godly Woman
By Carolyn Clare Givens

Strength and dignity are her clothing,
and she laughs at the time to come.
(Proverbs 31:25)

Dear Challenger, if you're anything like me, the idea of another devotional on the Proverbs 31 woman just made you gag a little bit. Don't worry; I've been to all the women's events where she's held up as a paragon of something I'm not and left feeling more than a little cynical about her—or rather, at what I've been told she is.

But take a moment to read Proverbs 31:10–31 and gain some insight about this *"excellent wife"* (verse 10). Many Bible translations have the heading "The Woman Who Fears the Lord" for these verses. This is no wilting flower of a woman. She is trusted and does good; she seeks, works, brings food, rises, provides, considers, buys, plants, dresses, makes strong, perceives profit, spins, reaches out, speaks wisdom, and teaches kindness. *"Strength and dignity are her clothing, and she laughs at the time to come"* (verse 25).

I love that image. What a picture of confidence: she laughs at the future. Displaying confidence is something that can come hard, even for Eights. Sometimes we've been shut down when we've done so. Sometimes we've seen our confidence fill a room and suck out the air for everyone else. We're overcoming a lot of doubts when we choose to laugh at the future, even if we'd never let anyone know it.

But for the Proverbs 31 woman, the future is not a fearful prospect, but an adventure. This woman knows her place—and that place is that of a businesswoman, an artist, a philanthropist, a protector, and a caretaker. She looks forward to what lies ahead for her because she knows she does none of these things in her own strength. Her confidence is not in herself, her charm, or her beauty. Instead, she fears the Lord, and it is His strength that gives her confidence. She can laugh at the future because He holds it in His hands.

SHIFT IN FOCUS

Ask God to show you the places where you can lean into His strength instead of your own. How can that shift make you more confident to be yourself?

Do you hesitate to live in your natural confidence? Review Proverbs 31 and ask God to show you yourself in some aspect of this godly woman. No one will be all the things she is—she's an ideal of wisdom—but in what areas is God calling you to walk forward confidently?

DAY 36 • • • • • • • • • • •

God Made You Purposefully

Before I formed you in the womb I knew you, and before you were born I consecrated you; I appointed you a prophet to the nations. (Jeremiah 1:5)

Before you were even born, God decided the world needed Eights. In Zechariah 10:3–5, we see this beautiful picture of God telling the people He would rise up to restore Judah and Israel:

> *My anger is hot against the shepherds, and I will punish the leaders; for the LORD of hosts cares for his flock, the house of Judah, and will make them like his majestic steed in battle. From him shall come the cornerstone, from him the tent peg, from him the battle bow, from him every ruler—all of them together. They shall be like mighty men in battle, trampling the foe in the mud of the streets; they shall fight because the LORD is with them, and they shall put to shame the riders on horses.*

The people of Israel were being led astray by their leaders, and God was not happy. He says that He will provide new leaders for His people, and under their leadership, His people shall become like steeds in battle.

These leaders will be a cornerstone—meaning they will be establishers. They will be a tent peg—meaning they will be strong and sturdy. They will be a battle bow—meaning they will be skilled in combat. These mighty men of battle will be strong because God will be with them and lend them His strength.

Dear Eight, God designed you with great purpose in mind. He did not design you by chance or mistake. He already has every page of your life penned out, and before you were even formed in your mother's womb, He knew you.

Part of the pain of having different personalities is that we can't always see and appreciate everyone's unique giftings, but God sees them all, and He is who decided you were needed right here, right now.

Don't insult your very Designer by questioning your design. You may not deliver an entire people group from captivity and rebuild God's church, but God has your own version of purpose designed just for you. You need only to walk in obedience and trust that your strength comes from Him.

SHIFT IN FOCUS

Do you struggle to appreciate your design?

It can be very hard to be a female Eight in America because it seems like this country was built on the foundation of Enneagram Two females and Enneagram Three males. Female Eights may feel out of place or "too much," but God knows you are anything but.

DAY 37 • • • • • • • • • • • •

How God Uses Your "Intimidation"

And let us not grow weary of doing good,
for in due season we will reap, if we do not give up.
(Galatians 6:9)

Do a quick Google search of "people who have changed the world."

Although we can't know these people's Enneagram numbers for sure, we see a lot of themes that feel Eight-ish and Five-ish. We have the crusaders, military officials, and fighters—people who changed the world with their hands: Eights. And we find the engineers, philosophers, and inventors—people who changed the world with their minds: Fives.

Although any type can change the world, using your hands or mind to do so feels distinctly Eight-ish and Five-ish. Eights and Fives share a vein of passion that doesn't let them live peacefully and die.

Eights can truly change the world, and you can see from your Google search that I'm not just saying that to flatter you. You might not even know your impact in your lifetime, but with our big God and your big passion—or what others may call intimidation—you can do a lot of good in your short time here on earth.

God uses even our biggest pain points to grow us, shape us, and change the world around us. What might seem like a burden we are carrying might be the very thing that becomes a strength in the right moment. God is big enough to do that, and I trust that you will see good come of your "intimidating" presence.

SHIFT IN FOCUS

Which person from your Google search stood out to you the most?

What did you learn that you didn't know before?

Invite God to convict you to act and be bold, trusting that He goes before you and is with you always.

DAY 38 • • • • • • • • • • •

Confidence on Display
By Carolyn Clare Givens

*Barak said to her, "If you will go with me, I will go, but if you will
not go with me, I will not go." And she said, "I will surely go with
you. Nevertheless, the road on which you are going will not lead to
your glory, for the LORD will sell Sisera into the hand of a woman."
Then Deborah arose and went with Barak to Kedesh.*
(Judges 4:8–9)

The book of Judges is full of some very interesting stories, and
the story of Deborah and Barak's war against Sisera is no excep-
tion. Deborah is a prophetess and judge over Israel. When she
calls on Barak to obey God and go up against their enemy in
battle, he says he'll only go if she goes with him. She agrees...
but tells him that because of his hesitation, God will deliver their
enemy into the hands of a woman.

And so it is: Sisera flees from the battle, and a woman named
Jael invites him into her tent, allowing him to believe that she
is an ally. She gives him milk to drink and a place to lie down
and rest. Then she picks up a tent peg and hammer and drives it
through his temple while he sleeps.

As Barak pursues Sisera, Jael catches him on the road. She
says, *"Come, and I will show you the man whom you are seeking"*
(Judges 4:22), and shows him Sisera's body.

It's a violent story—and I'm awfully glad we live under the
grace of the new covenant thanks to Jesus, rather than in the days

of the judges—but Deborah and Jael are incredible role models nonetheless. Both of them recognized their own strength.

Deborah was willing to be a leader and stands tall among the judges of Israel as one of the few we remember for her greatness rather than any foolishness. Remember Gideon, Jephthah, and Samson? They're some of the more familiar judges, and while God used them to lead Israel, they are also remembered for their weakness and faithlessness. Deborah, on the other hand, sat as a patient and wise judge over Israel and then rose up to lead the people into a victorious battle against their enemies.

Jael was smart. She recognized that Sisera would trust her because of the peace between his king and her husband, but she also knew that he was evil and bent on Israel's destruction. So she wooed him and offered him the illusion of safety before she dispatched him. She played the hand she was given and leveraged it for victory.

SHIFT IN FOCUS

Read Judges 4.

Do you think you will be remembered for your confidence and strength, like Deborah and Jael were?

Take a moment and reflect on the areas of your life where your strength has been called out by others. Do you prioritize those areas where your strength shines most?

DAY 39 • • • • • • • • • •

When You Feel Like You're Too Much

*Now to him who is able to do far more abundantly than
all that we ask or think, according to the power at work within
us, to him be glory in the church and in Christ Jesus
throughout all generations, forever and ever. Amen.*
(Ephesians 3:20–21)

Enneagram Fours, Sixes, and Eights all struggle with feeling like
they're *too much.* This is because they are all part of the reactive
conflict triad. They all want to feel heard and understood, particularly when conflicts arise. If others truly grasped our intentions,
there would be no need for the conflict in the first place, right? It
hurts when we feel misunderstood, especially by those who love
us. We react when others have a mistaken impression about us,
and other types tend to experience that reaction as *a lot* or *too
much.*

If you look back on your life, you may find it eerie to see
how your feeling misunderstood is connected to your feeling like
you're *too much* for people.

As an Enneagram Four myself, I know what it's like to feel
like you're too much. It causes you to hide parts of yourself and
try to fit into a mold that was never made for you. It can cause
you to envy those who are *just right,* and leaves its share of bruises
and scars.

Often the reality behind others' judgment is that they do
not feel the freedom to express themselves the way you do. They

think they aren't allowed to assert themselves, so why should you be able to? You must be doing something wrong.

The good news is that this is not how God experiences us. Our most chaotic, emotional, and messy moments are never too much for Him. He is patient with us, understanding, and is not surprised by who we are, even when we ourselves are.

God is too concerned with our eternal future to worry about our reputation here on earth. He doesn't care what Catherine thinks of you or what Rick said. He wants our eyes to be fixed on Him, and in Him is the humility to walk in our too-muchness.

SHIFT IN FOCUS

What is one area in your life or relationships where you constantly are feeling like you're too much?

Spend some time in prayer. What does God want you to know about how He sees you in that space?

DAY 40 • • • • • • • • • • •

How to Respond to Those Who Are Intimidated by You
By Carolyn Clare Givens

Do nothing from selfish ambition or conceit, but in humility count
others more significant than yourselves. Let each of you look
not only to his own interests, but also to the interests of others.
Have this mind among yourselves, which is yours in Christ Jesus,
who, though he was in the form of God, did not count equality with
God a thing to be grasped, but emptied himself, by taking the form
of a servant, being born in the likeness of men.
And being found in human form, he humbled himself by becoming
obedient to the point of death, even death on a cross.
(Philippians 2:3–8)

Dear Challenger, it can be really hard to figure out how to be wholly yourself when those around you are intimidated by you. Our go-to response tends to be one of actively seeking to be *less*. But just yesterday we looked at the lie that we are *too much*. And it's just that: a lie.

So how do we respond when those around us are intimidated? Every situation will be different, of course. It will help everyone if we go in with eyes open, prepared to read the responses of those we interact with and adjust. But adjusting doesn't necessarily mean dialing back.

In Philippians, Paul reminds us of a key factor in Christian community: humility. He calls us to adopt the same attitude as

Jesus, to *"in humility count others as more significant"* than our-selves (verse 3). And he reminds us that the King of Kings *"did not count equality with God a thing to be grasped"* (verse 6).

Scholars and theologians have spent two thousand years trying to figure out what the phrase *"emptied himself"* really means. We're not going to figure it out today. But I do love the Bible translation that tells us that Jesus *"made himself of no repu-tation"* (Philippians 2:7 KJV).

Humility is not lessening who I am; it is not "emptying" myself of my identity. Humility is counting myself—my repu-tation and my rights—as less important than those around me. So when I'm with someone who finds me intimidating, how can I count them as more significant than myself? When I'm in a situa-tion where I realize I'm taking up all the air in the room, how can I let go of my reputation and my rights to serve the people around me? In other words, how can I have the mind of Jesus?

SHIFT IN FOCUS

May this poem "Indwelling" by Thomas Edward Brown be an encouraging reminder that you are indwelled by the most gra-cious and humble King of the universe:

> If thou couldst empty all thyself of self,
>
> Like to a shell dishabited,
>
> Then might He find thee on the Ocean shelf,
>
> And say—"This is not dead,"—
>
> And fill thee with Himself instead.

But thou art all replete with very thou

And hast such shrewd activity,

That, when He comes, He says, "This is enow

Unto itself—'Twere better let it be:

It is so small and full, there is no room for Me."[4]

4. Thomas Edward Brown, "Indwelling," in *Old John and Other Poems* (London: MacMillan and Co., 1893), 151.

10 DAYS OF WITHDRAWING

Going to Five in Stress

• • • • • • • • • • • ## DAY 41

Seasons of Life

For everything there is a season, and a time for every matter under heaven: a time to be born, and a time to die; a time to plant, and a time to pluck up what is planted; a time to kill, and a time to heal; a time to break down, and a time to build up; a time to weep, and a time to laugh; a time to mourn, and a time to dance; a time to cast away stones, and a time to gather stones together; a time to embrace, and a time to refrain from embracing; a time to seek, and a time to lose; a time to keep, and a time to cast away; a time to tear, and a time to sew; a time to keep silence, and a time to speak; a time to love, and a time to hate; a time for war, and a time for peace.

(Ecclesiastes 3:1–8)

In the whirlwind of life, expectations, and demands, it can be hard to think of ourselves as living seasonally. We live on an earth with winter, spring, summer, and fall, and we observe and celebrate the earth and its seasons, but we rarely give ourselves permission to change and transform. Instead, we expect all or nothing. Either I am…or I am not. There is *right now*, and anything worth doing is worth doing *today*. This is especially true in the hustle of North America.

Of course, as we look at our own life, seasons are evident. There was that really hard year of illness, there were years of singleness, there were those amazing three months of falling in love, there were years with little kids, there were years of learning—everything in its own season.

We have a lot to learn from the way God created the earth with its seasons. In these verses from Ecclesiastes, Solomon notes there is a season for everything, and we can see that he's talking about us, not just the earth. The wisest king who ever lived says that for every bad or hard season we experience, there is a season of rest and good to come.

SHIFT IN FOCUS

In the next nine days, we will go into detail about what a season of growth looks like for you as an Eight.

As you look at your own life today, what season are you in? Read Ecclesiastes 3:1–8 again and pick one or two verbs that represent the season you're currently in.

Are you mourning, or celebrating?

Are you transitioning, or resting?

Are you uprooting, or planting?

If you're in a more hopeful, joyful, and restful season, it may be time to press into growth and celebrate the growth you can see in yourself. If you're in a season of difficulty, transition, and survival, it will be helpful for you to see this time as just a season, and see the hope on the horizon. You may even see some ways that you're growing even in stress and adversity.

Celebrate those wins!

DAY 42 • • • • • • • • • • •

What Is a Season of Stress?

Blessed is the man who remains steadfast under trial,
for when he has stood the test he will receive the crown of life,
which God has promised to those who love him.
(James 1:12)

In light of talking about seasons of life, we have to talk about the seasons of stress we walk through. Some are lighter than others, but all bring the anxiety and feeling of trying to survive that's familiar to us all. These are hard seasons.

When we talk about stress using Enneagram verbiage, we aren't talking about being late for work or losing your keys. We all get frustrated and irritable in those circumstances. No, when the Enneagram refers to stress, it means seasonal stress—you just lost your job, you're transitioning, your loved one just passed, and other harsh and trying circumstances. In those times, you're often in survival mode for months or years. This is the season of stress we are talking about.

A season of stress works like holding a pitcher that fills slowly or quickly, depending on the severity of stress. Once it's filled to the brim, these stress behaviors spill out. You won't be acting out of these behaviors all the time during a stressful season, but you may see a pattern of them spilling out periodically as you try to cope with stress.

For Eights, during periods of seasonal stress, you'll start to exhibit unhealthy behaviors of Fives. You may lose energy and withdraw. All of a sudden, you're fixated and focused on something that isolates you from others.

These behaviors should work as a stoplight for you to ask yourself a few questions:

+ What is stressing me out right now?

+ Am I currently in a season of stress?

+ If I could look back on "me in stress" in another season, how would I be kinder to myself?

+ Where should I be resting or giving myself more grace during this season?

Seasons of stress are nothing to be ashamed of. If anything, they cause us to cling to God in a really precious way and become highly aware of our need for Him.

SHIFT IN FOCUS

Take a couple of moments to reflect on the season you're in right now. Is this a season of growth for you, or a season of stress?

If it's a season of stress for you, take a deep breath, be kind to your battered heart, and cling to the Lord.

Steadfastness under trial is honoring to God, but that doesn't mean we should pretend there is no trial.

DAY 43 • • • • • • • • • • •

The Worst of Type Five

Whoever isolates himself seeks his own desire;
he breaks out against all sound judgment.
(Proverbs 18:1)

Fives worry deep down that they don't have what it takes in order to do their job, provide for themselves and their family, or function in the world. This is why they'll spend the majority of their lives pursuing competency: to silence these fears of inadequacy. Fives' need for competency is one of the reasons they avoid social situations, as small talk can make them feel unprepared.

Without the feeling of competency, Fives:

+ Fear humiliation and failure

+ Feel like they're a waste of space

+ Often become depressed

Average slightly unhealthy Fives will need a lot of time to process and think things through before acting. They may experience a fair amount of social anxiety. Average Fives won't view themselves as being isolated, but they will rarely accept a spontaneous invitation; instead, they tend to hoard their time and energy. Feeling the need to have strong personal opinions can cause average Fives to become unintentionally argumentative and negative. Sensing others don't put the same amount of thought as they do into any given subject, average Fives will often come off as arrogant.

When I read anything about very unhealthy Fives, I can't help but picture Ted Kaczynski, the Unabomber loner whose nationwide bombing campaign targeted people whom he believed were promoting technology and hurting the environment. Although we don't know his Enneagram type, unhealthy Fives will often become textbook recluses. With only themselves to fact check their thought life, they often fall prey to odd or extreme ideas. They'll demonize social structure and purposely push people away by being mean and argumentative. At their most unhealthy, Fives will become highly unstable and may suffer from schizophrenia.

It may feel a bit funny to be talking so much about a Five in a devotional meant for Eights, but because you do go to Five in stress, I want you to have a detailed look into what this type looks like. I could give you a list of behaviors that might be possible for you as you move to Five in stress, but I could never think of all the practical ways this could play out for you.

So I encourage you, as you feel stressed, to look at what wanting to look competent and withdrawing look like for you.

SHIFT IN FOCUS

+ Do you know any Enneagram Fives?

+ What is hard for you about them?

+ When do you notice yourself withdrawing most?

DAY 44 • • • • • • • • • • • •

How Do I Go to Five?

For nothing is hidden that will not be made manifest, nor is
anything secret that will not be known and come to light.
(Luke 8:17)

Stressed out Eights report feeling quiet and unmotivated. They shut down and shut up while internally they're experiencing an emotional tsunami.

Being emotional feels vulnerable, and you might struggle to keep your walls up, so you retreat to feel safe. If you can't deal with the feelings, you might indulge in mind-numbing behaviors to distract yourself from feeling them at all.

Going to Five can mean picking up their withdrawing, quiet, and often obsessive tendencies. Have you ever shut yourself away for days and busted out a project that didn't *need* to happen right then? You were probably stressed.

Have you ever isolated yourself, not wanting to talk to anyone—even those you love—instead seeking to be alone for days on end? You were probably in a season of stress.

Have you ever watched TV, played video games, surfed the Internet, or eaten junk food well into the night, even into the early morning hours, all alone? You were probably stressed.

Have others told you that you weren't acting like your "normal, energetic self"? You were probably stressed.

In stressful situations, do you become uncharacteristically quiet and feel like a failure because you just want to be alone and shut down instead of caring for everyone else who is hurting in the same situation?

These are all very normal stress behaviors for Eights.

For someone who is on the go most of the time, it can be staggering to find yourself no longer active and interested in life, but isolated and feeling blah instead. But it happens, dear Eight, when you go to Five in stress. When you are aware of these seismic shifts in your temperament, it's much easier to find your path forward.

SHIFT IN FOCUS

Where are you most tempted to hide today?

Do you spend alone time mind-numbing when emotions get too loud?

What is your mind-numbing behavior of choice?

What might it look like to openly process that emotion when you're alone instead of turning to mind-numbing behaviors?

DAY 45 • • • • • • • • • • •

What I'm Actually Longing For

Have I not commanded you? Be strong and courageous.
Do not be frightened, and do not be dismayed, for the
LORD your God is with you wherever you go.
(Joshua 1:9)

Dear Challenger, when you feel the toll of a season of stress, you may start to feel quiet and more emotionally vulnerable. This happens as you feel control slipping through your fingers, with seemingly no ability to take back the reins.

As an Eight, you have developed coping skills to try to keep yourself and others safe. However, the coping skills you gain from going to Five in stress provide more of an avoiding and withdrawing approach to the outside world than actually providing emotional, spiritual, and physical safety.

In seasons of stress, you as an Eight *need to feel safe*, and when nothing's in your control, you tend to feel anything but. Leaning on and trusting in the Lord during this time might feel impossibly hard, but constantly reminding yourself who is really in control is the only thing that will help you feel safe. As we see in Joshua 1:9, the reason God gives Joshua for being courageous, not frightened or dismayed, is that *"the LORD your God is with you wherever you go."*

You cannot travel out of His sight, and no situation you get yourself into is beyond His control.

In today's Scripture reading, Moses had died and it was up to his assistant, Joshua, to lead the people into the promised land. We don't know if Joshua was frightened or feeling under pressure, but we do know that for whatever reason, God reassured Israel's new leader several times that He was with them and Joshua needed to be *"strong and courageous."* (See Joshua 1:1–9.)

No matter what difficulties we are going through, nothing can separate us from God and His love. As Paul tells the church in Rome:

> *For I am sure that neither death nor life, nor angels nor rulers, nor things present nor things to come, nor powers, nor height nor depth, nor anything else in all creation, will be able to separate us from the love of God in Christ Jesus our Lord.* (Romans 8:38–39)

It may seem odd to be longing for safety in moments of disappointment, frustration, and stress, but all of those feelings expose that you are not truly in control here and consequently make you feel unsafe. However, like a child, when you trust who is in control, you can be set at ease. You can rest in peace knowing that God's hand is what holds your life, and you can use these Five tendencies for recharging and truly resting instead of isolating.

SHIFT IN FOCUS

Fear is a funny thing to wrestle with as an adult. I think we all assume our years of feeling "not in control" and fearful will be solved when we are in the driver's seat. However, God has a way of showing us just how little control we have over our circumstances, especially in adulthood.

What's the last situation you were in that truly made you feel unsafe?

Spend some time in prayer and ask God for an image of how He was with you then. An image will be helpful for you to be able to bring to memory the next time you feel even a glimmer of that same emotion.

• • • • • • • • • • • DAY 46

How Five-ness Is Trying to Help
By Carolyn Clare Givens

Six days shall work be done, but on the seventh day is a Sabbath
of solemn rest, a holy convocation. You shall do no work. It is a
Sabbath to the LORD in all your dwelling places.
(Leviticus 23:3)

Dear Challenger, have you ever heard the phrase "scarcity mindset"? It's a psychological concept that says there is a finite amount of resources and therefore you must be careful in how you use them. In contrast, an abundance mindset sees that there is enough out there for everyone, and thus resources can be used without fear that they will run out.

Often, our Eight-ness tends toward an abundance mindset. We know that we have plenty of strength, and we expect that the resources around us are probably more bountiful than anyone realizes. And so we power on through without any thought of conservation.

Fives, on the other hand, tend toward a scarcity mindset. As an Eight, when we are in stress, we can land in that mindset that our resources are few and we must hold onto what we have. This might be just what we need: something in our internal makeup that says, "Wait, stop, rest. Hold on. You don't know if more energy will come tomorrow, so don't use up the last ounce of it today."

Here's the crazy thing, though: God turns the whole thing upside down with the idea of *Sabbath*. The Sabbath of the Old Testament law was a command from God that after six days of work, the seventh day would be a day of rest without work.

For an Eight, the idea of a *Sabbath* can feel constraining. This is where our Five-ness can help: regular rhythms of rest are beneficial and centering. But the Sabbath also resists our scarcity mindsets because God is saying, "Trust me for one day. I will provide for you, and you will have enough."

As we move forward into the New Testament, Jesus calls himself Lord of the Sabbath and reminds us that He is the source of our rest. *"Come to me, all who labor and are heavy laden, and I will give you rest"* (Matthew 11:28).

SHIFT IN FOCUS

In what areas of your life do you need to lean into the scarcity mindset of your Five-ness and take your foot off the gas?

In what areas of your life do you need to lean into God's provision for you, rather than working for all of your accomplishments?

• • • • • • • • • • • DAY 47

The Temptation of Withdrawing

Do not be anxious about anything, but in everything by prayer and supplication with thanksgiving let your requests be made known to God. And the peace of God, which surpasses all understanding, will guard your hearts and your minds in Christ Jesus.
(Philippians 4:6–7)

Having a *tendency* to withdraw and *being* withdrawn are two different things. As an Eight, you have a tendency to withdraw in stress, but this doesn't change who you are at the core.

The Enneagram teaches us that there are three different stances or attitudes that define our social style of how we get what we need or want. Fives are part of the withdrawn stance; they move away from others. In practice, this stance looks something like this: when they are overcharged for something at a store, instead of speaking up, a Five will just pay...and never go back to that establishment again.

It might be hard for you to understand that, as you are part of the aggressive stance, along with Threes and Sevens. This means you will most likely say something if you are being overcharged. But the withdrawn stance is the reality for Fives, Fours, and Nines. If something goes wrong, they don't trust that they can affect their environment, so if they're upset, instead of actually doing something about it, they'll just go away and not let it happen again.

When it comes to loud sadness, feeling unsafe, hopeless, and everything else stress can bring, you may arrive at this point. You feel you can no longer do anything about your issues or problems, and you're done trying—so you remove yourself from the situation.

Withdrawing can be an affair lasting a couple of hours, or you might wake up a month from now not remembering the last time you left your house. But either way, this becomes a big temptation for you in stress.

It's important to remember that coping mechanisms are trying to help you, but they don't often deliver on their promises. When you realize that you have withdrawn and you're conserving your energy, it is a good time to check in with yourself and see how resting, for a set amount of time, would be helpful.

One of the keys to help you avoid withdrawing in a sinful, self-serving, and destructive way is to communicate your intentions to those around you and set boundaries for withdrawing from them. This is as simple as saying, "I think I need to go watch TV for an hour and recharge. If you need me, you know where I'll be."

Disappearing on those who love you is not kind, but it's amazing how hard communicating can be when you feel overwhelmed by Five-ness in stress. You're going to have to decide in advance that this is important for you to do and create a plan.

SHIFT IN FOCUS

What is something that makes you feel rested?

What is a reasonable amount of time for you to do this activity?

Who is the most important person for you to tell when you need to withdraw?

Your answer to these three questions is what, how long, and to whom you need to communicate to guard yourself against disappearing. This is your game plan for when you need to rest and withdraw with boundaries.

DAY 48 • • • • • • • • • • •

The Temptation of Numbing
By Carolyn Clare Givens

*The discerning sets his face toward wisdom, but the
eyes of a fool are on the ends of the earth.*
(Proverbs 17:24)

Dear Challenger, when you're tired and worn, stressed and spent, how do you respond? One of the simplest and most tempting responses is to separate yourself emotionally and mentally from normal life and find somewhere else to go inside your head.

This might mean physical activity for you, it might mean binge-watching a TV show, or it could be consuming an excess of alcohol or food, or any one of a number of other ways that we find to numb ourselves. Navigating the line of what is a healthy break from the stresses of every day and what is numbing ourselves is a constant challenge and not one easily answered.

Throughout Proverbs, we are faced with the actions of "a fool" in contrast to the actions of one who seeks wisdom. The fool runs his mouth, trusts his own mind, and is hasty in his decisions. The wise man is circumspect, cautious, and seeks knowledge and discernment.

Numbing is often tempting simply *because* it has no point. There's not a goal or focus to it, and therefore it serves as a rest from our need to push toward our accomplishments. But "*the eyes of a fool are on the ends of the earth"* (Proverbs 17:24). The fool's numbing points him everywhere except toward wisdom.

In Proverbs 9, Wisdom, personified as a woman, works hard, sets a table, and invites all to come to it. She provides for the simple and naïve. She says, *"Leave your simple ways, and live, and walk in the way of insight"* (verse 6). A few verses later, we are introduced to another woman, Folly, who seduces the simpleton to his death. *"To him who lacks sense she says, 'Stolen water is sweet, and bread eaten in secret is pleasant'"* (verses 16–17).

When we are tempted to numb, we need the Lord's help to seek wisdom instead of folly. Set your face toward Him.

SHIFT IN FOCUS

What ways have you learned to discern the difference between taking a break and falling into a numbing activity?

What are your go-to numbing activities? Find someone to hold you accountable for how you approach these.

Ask God to help you seek wisdom over folly.

DAY 49 • • • • • • • • • • •

The Temptation of Isolating

*If anyone is caught in any transgression, you who are spiritual
should restore him in a spirit of gentleness....Bear one
another's burdens, and so fulfill the law of Christ*
(Galatians 6:1–2)

Withdrawing and isolating are two very different things.
Withdrawing is something you will feel the urge to do whether
there is some major family drama going on or you were involved
in a minor car accident and become stressed over the cost of
fixing your car.

Isolating is physically separating from the world and discon-
necting emotionally, mentally, and spiritually. What you do and
where you go in isolation is going to be different for every Eight,
but the goal is the same: "I feel weak, and if I show up, people will
notice and take advantage of me."

My prayer is that isolation events will be few and far between
in your life. There are usually only a couple of occasions in an
Eight's life where they truly feel weak, but it does happen. And
these occasions normally have to do with the death of someone
close to them.

Isolation is the defensive mechanism most often used by
Fives. They isolate to protect themselves and their energy stores
from the world. Fives can detach and live in isolation for years;
this is often their preferred method of living if they don't feel

appreciated, respected, or *enough* for those in their life. All they need is the means to disappear, and they will.

Have you ever *disappeared?* It might be hard to think of a time you've done this if no one had to send out a search party for you, but it's likely that you have hidden yourself away in one way or another.

The biggest problem with isolating is that, although it is protecting yourself from looking weak in front of those whose respect you desire, you are not allowing your fellow Christians to live in community with you and help to bear your burdens, as Paul encourages us in today's Scripture reading.

God did not make us to live in isolation at the expense of our relationships. From the beginning of creation, we have been made to live harmoniously with other people. God said of Adam's isolated state, *"It is not good that the man should be alone"* (Genesis 2:18). And that echoes through all of us who are created, like Adam, to need each other not just in a marital sense but in a communal one as well.

We need community, we need each other, and even if we show up weak, God is still glorified. (See 2 Corinthians 12:9–11.)

SHIFT IN FOCUS

Think about your community: your family, church, work-place, neighborhood, and other groups to which you belong.

How can you see God's faithfulness, love, and good design played out in those relationships?

When you feel the temptation to isolate, it's good to reflect on this question. These people are God's hands and feet to help you, love you, and comfort you. Depriving them of the chance to help you bear your burdens not only hinders their spiritual growth, but it ultimately hurts you.

• • • • • • • • • • • • DAY 50

How to Survive Stress Out in the Open

Do not be anxious about anything, but in everything by prayer and supplication with thanksgiving let your requests be made known to God. And the peace of God, which surpasses all understanding, will guard your hearts and your minds in Christ Jesus.
(Philippians 4:6–7)

Seasons of stress are unique and hard times for us all. No matter whether the season is short or long, we feel the strain it has placed on us and long for relief. We think:

+ *I just need to get to next month.*

+ *Things will be okay if I get a new job.*

+ *If this situation improves just a little, I'll have some hope to cling to.*

You may need to get over this hump in order to be okay, but for right now, you're here—and you need to be kind to yourself.

Being kind to yourself means tending to your relationships and not burning bridges by isolating yourself. It means telling people that you're stressed, communicating what that looks like for you, and allowing them to pray and check in. It looks like doing the uncomfortable work of figuring out *what* you're feeling, *why* you're feeling that way, and letting yourself work through those emotions without dismissing them.

It can be helpful to look at yourself with the eyes of a future you, two years from now. What will you be proud you did, and what will you wish you hadn't spent as much time beating yourself up about?

One of the reasons it can be hard to fight negative stress behaviors is because we are still trying to do it all and keep the status quo, even though our current season is not set up for that.

If your family is in transition—with a new baby, moving, a marriage or divorce—you're surviving.

If you just got fired, you're surviving.

If you lost someone close to you, then you're surviving.

You in stress and you in growth aren't going to be the same. In stress, you won't be able to handle the same amount of *life* and do all the same things as you would in growth, and that's not a failure on your part. We all go through seasons where we just can't take on as much, but in our pride, we often almost kill ourselves trying to paint a different picture to everyone who's watching. No one has it all together, and everyone goes through seasons of stress. We are not all or nothing; we are seasonal beings who go through trials, changes, and all manner of suffering.

Forcing the same expectations on yourself when you're stressed as you do in a growth season will only lead to burnout and disappointment.

SHIFT IN FOCUS

If you're currently in a season of stress, what needs to be put on the back burner until later? Name three things that can wait:

1. _____
_____

2. _____
_____

3. _____
_____

Who needs to know about the stress you're under? Name three people who could benefit from this knowledge or who could help you:

1._____

2._____

3._____

Where are your expectations for yourself not matching your reality?

If you're not in a season of stress:

+ Write a letter to future stressed-out you.

+ Try to identify a couple of people around you who are going through a season of stress. How can you be praying for and supporting them?

10 DAYS OF VULNERABILITY

Going to Two in Growth

• • • • • • • • • • • **DAY 51**

Seasons of Growth

> *Every good gift and every perfect gift is from above,*
> *coming down from the Father of lights, with whom there is no*
> *variation or shadow due to change.*
> (James 1:17)

As we talked about in the beginning of our conversation about stress, thinking of your life in seasonal terms is not only biblical, but it also gives you a lot more grace and hope for your circumstances. Seasons of stress are the opposite of seasons of growth. The latter are periods in your life in which you feel as if you have room to breathe, have more energy, and can focus on spiritual, mental, and physical growth.

Seasons of growth are often blurry or over-romanticized when we look back at our life as a whole. We either can't remember a time in our life that we didn't feel the hum of anxiety and stress, or we can't live fully in the present because no season will ever be as good as it has been in the past.

Both of these thought processes are unfruitful because they're extremes. There is always a mixture of good and bad in every situation; only the details change. This is a result of living in a fallen world. We are living outside of our natural habitat, and it often feels like a paradox of good and bad at the same time.

Now, this doesn't mean that seasons of stress and growth coexist all the time; often, they don't. Circumstances in our lives often tip the scales. Nothing is ever all bad or all good. Working in a toxic environment or the death of a loved one will send us into a season of stress. Likewise, getting our dream job, hitting a sweet spot with parenting, or flourishing in a good friendship can tip the scale to seasons of growth.

You should push yourself during seasons of growth. Have you been wanting to read a certain book or join a Bible study? Do it! Are you thinking about starting a diet or exercising more? Now's the time! We literally have more mental space, more energy, and more bandwidth when we are in seasons of growth.

We can also see a lot of encouraging behaviors pop up. Press into them and build them in a way that they'll stick beyond this season. Create good habits that will serve a future, stressed-out you. Consistent Bible reading is a must for all of life, but especially those hard days when you feel lost.

Growth seasons are the days of digging deep and reaping the rewards. These seasons are a gift from a heavenly Father who loves you and wants to give you good things.

The apostle Peter tells us:

As each has received a gift, use it to serve one another, as good stewards of God's varied grace. (1 Peter 4:10)

We should be using these seasons of *good gifts* to not only build up our faith, but also to help others. In the next nine days, you'll see how going to Two in growth helps you specifically with this.

SHIFT IN FOCUS

Are you currently in a season of growth?

Do you have a couple of good seasons in your past that you might be over-romanticizing, or maybe feel ungrateful for?

DAY 52 • • • • • • • • • • •

How Do I Go to Two?

Let each of you look not only to his own interests,
but also to the interests of others.
(Philippians 2:4)

The practicalities of going to Two in growth can feel hard to grasp when most of the information about Twos makes them seem soft, motherly, and maybe even weak. But the strongest parts of Twos are areas where you, as an Eight, will tend to be weakest.

LISTENING

Listening thoughtfully is not often a strength of those who are future-focused and action-oriented. You may get frustrated with people who seem to overshare and over-communicate when you'd prefer them to just get to the point. However, when you go to Two in growth, it'll be easier for you to listen intently and stay present in the conversation.

FORESEEING NEEDS

You may be gifted in foreseeing the practical needs of those around you, but what about their emotional needs? What emotional support does your child need on their first day of school? What can you do to help a friend through a breakup? Are you prepared to stay with them in the emotion, walking with them through it, without dismissing them or trying to get them "over it"? As you go to Two in growth, foreseeing emotional needs will become clearer, and your ability to show up with people in that emotional time will also become easier.

VULNERABILITY

One of the dirtiest words, if you are an Eight, tends to be *vulnerability*. I know, I know—yuck! But hear me out. The greatest, scariest, and bravest moments in your life will require great vulnerability from you. Vulnerability means being susceptible to risk. In other words, taking off your armor. Trusting that God did not make your tender heart to be hidden and will heal your heart if it gets broken in the process of you trusting God enough to be vulnerable. This is one of the biggest areas Eights need to develop in order to grow, and it's a great gifting of type Twos.

SHIFT IN FOCUS

What area of Two-ness do you feel like you need to grow in the most this month?

In the past, which area have you really grown in?

DAY 53 • • • • • • • • • • • •

The Best of Type Two
By Christine Rollings

For we are his workmanship, created in Christ Jesus for good works, which God prepared beforehand, that we should walk in them.
(Ephesians 2:10)

The Enneagram teaches us that as Eights are growing, they will take on some of the healthy characteristics of a Two. By no means does this mean that you, as an Eight, become a Two or exhibit all the characteristics of a Two. You may notice a few key attributes of Twos that you find attractive. Perhaps you've been drawn to close friendship with a Two, admiring these things about them. And perhaps you've even named these things for yourself as areas in your life where you want to grow. That's all part of what it means to be an Enneagram Eight: that you do take on the best of type Two!

Healthy Twos are the glue that holds any community together. They're the friends seeing your needs and offering to help when you need it, listening to you with an open heart, and offering space to simply be. Twos who are healthy have learned a good balance of taking care of themselves as they also live out their gift of taking care of others.

While unhealthy to average Twos may want to fix things when people share with them, healthy Twos are able to listen without needing to offer advice or attempt to solve the problem. This is something you grow toward as well.

While unhealthy to average Twos may act on what they think another person needs and try to offer that to them, healthy Twos will be in tune with what that person really needs and learn to ask appropriately how they can help. This kind of action—not just seeing what you think others have, but being in tune with the real need and asking how you can help—is what growth for an Eight may look like. You put action to your anger, you actively and productively fight injustice, and you work out ways to push back against the darkness in our world!

As you move toward growth, your boldness in care for the people in your life is fierce and your attentiveness to what kind of care they need is clear. You move toward generosity with your time, your money, and your emotional resources. Growth for you looks like vulnerability with the trusted people in your life, being willing to show that you don't have it all together and trust that they value you for all you bring to the relationship.

SHIFT IN FOCUS

+ In which of these ways have you seen yourself grow?

+ In which of these ways would you like to grow?

DAY 54 • • • • • • • • • • • •

Why Do I Need Two-ness to Grow?

And I will give you a new heart, and a new spirit
I will put within you. And I will remove the heart of
tone from your flesh and give you a heart of flesh.
(Ezekiel 36:26)

When you were a child, you learned you could be betrayed and that people in general can't be trusted. In an act of protection, you decided, *I will never let anyone else control me*, and *I will protect myself from hurt*. These two promises to yourself have probably served you well, but in the process of protecting yourself, you may have also hardened your heart.

I see this all the time in the comments on my Instagram page @enneagram.life: "If I hurt you, you deserved it!" "No one can hurt me." "I don't care what anyone thinks of me!"

All of these comments are lies, but when you harden yourself, you can begin to believe they're really true.

I have had the privilege of watching a pastor, who may or may not be an Eight, throughout several years of his ministry. This pastor was tough and he seemed not to care what others thought of him. He was a man of action, and when he brought down the hammer, everyone felt it. As he grew into his pastorate, however, I saw a completely different side come out in him. He was still strong and action-oriented—and you definitely wouldn't want to cross him—but he was also gentle, tender, and wanted to make sure everyone felt heard. He was quick to apologize and didn't assume he was in the right. This is humility. This pastor's heart became softer, and his transformation brought glory to God.

This is what going to Two does for Eights. This growth doesn't change who you are made to be and your strengths, but Two-ness does make your approach more effective with others.

I know you don't want others to feel unheard, mowed over, or hurt, but having the patience to make people feel heard and loved will require softening your heart toward them. You're going to have to trust, be vulnerable, and slow down for this to happen.

> *Put on then, as God's chosen ones, holy and beloved, compassionate hearts, kindness, humility, meekness, and patience.*
> (Colossians 3:12)

SHIFT IN FOCUS

Do you have Twos in your life?

What do you admire about them?

In what ways has your heart already softened in your life?

DAY 55 • • • • • • • • • • • •

Grow in Listening
By Carolyn Clare Givens

Let every person be quick to hear, slow to speak, slow to anger; for the anger of man does not produce the righteousness of God.
(James 1:19–20)

Dear Challenger, what a gift our Two-ness can be when it comes to listening! Eights are rarely slow to do anything—we take in information, process, and act before anyone else can blink. But taking the time to slow down the reaction and be in the moment with someone is a gift, and an area in which we can definitely grow.

As your Sunday school teacher likely told you when you learned this verse from James, "You've got two ears and one mouth." It takes discipline, time, and energy to listen and remain in the moment with someone when they are sharing with you, but it's what we're meant to do in a community.

As an Eight, you're often seeking to protect and care for those you love, but how often do you stop to take the time to listen and hear what they really need? It's so much simpler to decide what's needed on our own and then fix it, right?

But let us be quick to listen so that we can really hear the hearts of those we love. Let us give our attention and empathize with what we hear. Let us not formulate a solution, but sit in the moment with our friend or loved one. So often it is the act of listening that is the most caring thing we can do.

Throughout Scripture, God's people are reminded to listen to Him—to His Word, His law, and His prophets, over and over again. And repeatedly, they fail to do so. Their failure pains and grieves God, but it destroys them. Had they only listened, they would have enjoyed the best of the land, but instead, they refused and rebelled, and lost the good gifts God had for them. (See Isaiah 1:18–20.)

SHIFT IN FOCUS

If this prayer speaks to your heart, please borrow it:

Dear heavenly Father, give me ears to hear and a heart to listen. Help me to still my tongue, my brain, my activity, and sit in the moment with the one I'm listening to. Help me to discern the meaning behind their words and serve them as best as I can in the ways they need. Amen.

DAY 56 • • • • • • • • • • •

Growing in Compassion
By Christine Rollings

Blessed be the God and Father of our Lord Jesus Christ,
the Father of mercies and God of all comfort, who comforts us
in all our affliction, so that we may be able to comfort those
who are in any affliction, with the comfort with which we
ourselves are comforted by God.
(2 Corinthians 1:3–4)

Yesterday, we talked about how Eights grow in listening as they tap into the healthy tendencies of a Two. As you grow in listening, taking the time to make space for others before trying to fix the situation or problem, God grows your heart in compassion for others.

Dear Challenger, you may jump at the chance to speak up or take concrete action against injustice in defense of those who are suffering. This is something we love about you! As a Two, I admire the determination and action of the Eights in my life and find myself cheering them on and being inspired and challenged by that boldness and bravery that comes so naturally to you.

The English word *compassion* comes from a Latin word that means "to suffer with." In the book *Compassion: A Reflection on the Christian Life*, Henri Noewen writes:

Compassion asks us to go where it hurts, to enter into
the places of pain, to share in brokenness, fear, confusion,

and anguish. Compassion challenges us to cry out with those in misery, to mourn with those who are lonely, to weep with those in tears. Compassion requires us to be weak with the weak, vulnerable with the vulnerable, and powerless with the powerless. Compassion means full immersion in the condition of being human.[5]

Sometimes the action that is required is simply being: spending time with a hurting person, or listening to a friend as their heart aches. Compassion looks like allowing our hearts to be broken alongside one another and places us in a position of vulnerability as we acknowledge our own weakness and inability to fix the situation. In your seasons of growth, dear Challenger, your heart leans into this surrender and stillness. Your tenderness is your strength as you mourn with those who mourn and rejoice with those who rejoice. (See Romans 12:15.)

SHIFT IN FOCUS

When has someone demonstrated compassion for you? What did it feel like to receive that compassion?

Where in your life does compassion feel the most natural? In what ways do you need to ask for the Lord's help to grow in compassion toward others? How can He help you grow in compassion toward yourself?

---

5. Henri J. M. Nouwen, Donald P. McNeill, and Douglas A. Morrison, *Compassion: A Reflection on the Christian Life* (New York: Image Books/Doubleday, 2006).

DAY 57 • • • • • • • • • • • •

Growing in Care
By Christine Rollings

*Let each of you look not only to his own interests, but also to the
interests of others. Have this mind among yourselves, which is yours
in Christ Jesus, who, though he was in the form of God, did not
count equality with God a thing to be grasped, but emptied himself,
by taking the form of a servant, being born in the likeness of men.*
(Philippians 2:4–7)

As Elisabeth mentioned at the beginning of this section, seasons of growth are times in our lives when we may have the energy and space to focus more on our own growth. We have more room spiritually, mentally, and physically to learn new things and take steps toward rhythms that may feel difficult in other seasons.

For you, dear Challenger, one of those ways you grow in these seasons is how you care for those around you. Enneagram Twos are known for their care of others, and as such, they're often referred to as "the Helper." As you go toward Two in this season, you grow in your capacity and ability to recognize the needs of the people in your life. Twos' helpfulness isn't just about the action of helping, but about their ability to see the needs of those around them and instinctively move to meet them.

It's likely that even in times that aren't seasons of growth, you are caring for others. So what makes this season different? Eights take care of their people too—and if a friend or family member asks you to do something, you often do it with joy.

Yet this growing season is a period of time when you have the bandwidth and natural capacity to give of yourself in deeper ways, and even without being asked. You will be able to see the needs of those around you and be more active in meeting them instinctively, whether that be lending a hand or offering a listening ear.

Paul instructs the early Christians at Philippi: *"Let each of you look not only to his own interests, but also to the interests of others."* This verse about caring for others offers us key insight into growth. He doesn't say that we shouldn't look out for our own interests, but that we shouldn't only look out for our own interests. It is important to care for ourselves so that we will be able to see others' needs and have the capacity to meet them.

SHIFT IN FOCUS

Here are some ideas for ways you can lean into growing in care when you are in a season of growth:

+ Reach out to a friend for coffee or a meal.

+ Verbalize to someone how much you care about them.

+ Do something to take care of yourself.

What's one way you can go the extra mile to care for someone in your life this week?

DAY 58 • • • • • • • • • • • •

Growing in Vulnerability
By Christine Rollings

But he said to me, "My grace is sufficient for you, for my power is made perfect in weakness." Therefore I will boast all the more gladly of my weaknesses, so that the power of Christ may rest upon me....For when I am weak, then I am strong.
(2 Corinthians 12:9–10)

Vulnerability can be a scary thing. You may have experienced past hurts in the moments you were brave enough to share deep parts of yourself. You may have felt misunderstood or had someone insist you said something that you did not say. You may have told yourself, "Never again." You may have had seasons in your life when your strength was a mask for that vulnerability.

As an Eight, when you move toward Two in seasons of growth, you grow toward seeing your vulnerability as a strength. In these times, you truly believe that people do not have the power to destroy you and you recognize that you are safe and protected in Christ. You embrace that divine protection, which means that even when others let you down or betray you, you know that God never will. He will not forsake or abandon you, and He delights in you as you rest in His strength and count it as your own.

Growing in vulnerability does not necessarily mean sharing your deepest self with everyone. There is wisdom in trusting your gut when it comes to knowing who or what is a safe and healthy relationship or situation. Growing in vulnerability does not mean throwing boundaries out the window; it does mean learning how to steward those boundaries and your vulnerability in relationships.

Vulnerability isn't an all or nothing state of being. You can choose the areas where you can take steps toward vulnerability, not sharing your full story but small snippets at a time when it feels safe to do so. It can feel hard to have another person not know the full context to your story, and there also can be a delight in the slow unraveling of your life experiences in friendship as another person becomes safe and trusted.

The vulnerability of trusting others and letting them care for you brings glory to God. He delights in seeing you share your story, whether that be all of it or small snippets, so that, as Paul tells the Corinthians, *"the power of Christ may rest"* upon us.

SHIFT IN FOCUS

Who are the people in your life with whom you feel safe enough to be vulnerable? Write their names here:

_____

_____

What is one small way you want to grow in vulnerability? What do you need to believe in order to take that step?

DAY 59 • • • • • • • • • • •

The Vulnerable Eight

*Who is weak, and I am not weak? Who is made to fall, and
I am not indignant? If I must boast, I will boast of the things that
show my weakness. The God and Father of the Lord Jesus,
he who is blessed forever, knows that I am not lying.*
(2 Corinthians 11:29–31)

Brené Brown is one of the first people in my life to point out
that bravery is seen as strength and vulnerability is classically
seen as weakness—but doesn't anything that requires bravery
also require vulnerability? If vulnerability means knowing you
could be hurt but moving forward anyway, then vulnerability is
bravery.

Brown told a *Forbes* writer:

> The difficult thing is that vulnerability is the first thing
> I look for in you and the last thing I'm willing to show
> you. In you, it's courage and daring. In me, it's weak-
> ness. This is where shame comes into play. Vulnerability
> is about showing up and being seen. It's tough to do
> that when we're terrified about what people might see
> or think. When we're fueled by the fear of what other
> people think or that gremlin that's constantly whisper-
> ing "You're not good enough" in our ear, it's tough to

show up. We end up hustling for our worthiness rather than standing in it.[6]

While for other Enneagram types, growth work is action, decisiveness, and confidence, for Eights, it's vulnerability. You have such a strong pulse on safety and protection that the risk of emotional vulnerability might never make sense to you. This is why you will have to train your mind to recognize its importance. In order to see its value, you will have to practice vulnerability and see the change it makes in your relationships.

You must bravely risk being seen as weak. You become human in weakness and, in the great paradox of life, you also become stronger and gain more respect.

Humility, vulnerability, and tenderness are the height of growth for Eights. When an Eight experiences these three things, we don't see them as weak; we see them as kind, sacrificial, and a beacon bringing glory to God.

When you are vulnerable, you're not losing your strength, but you're making everything you do for the glory of God more effective. People are going to be more willing to listen to your cause for justice if you're humble. People will be more likely to ask for your protection if you are tender. And people will be more likely to feel like they know you if you're vulnerable.

---

6. Dan Schawbel, "Brené Brown: How Vulnerability Can Make Our Lives Better," *Forbes*, April 21, 2013 (www.forbes.com/sites/danschawbel/2013/04/21/brene-brown-how-vulnerability-can-make-our-lives-better/?sh=7328d0a336c7).

This isn't always going to be a two-way street, and those you practice vulnerability with might not respond the way you would hope, but you can control yourself and your own growth.

SHIFT IN FOCUS

Who are the vulnerable people in your life? What can you learn from them?

Pray and ask God to help you figure out what practicing vulnerability looks like this week.

• • • • • • • • • • • **DAY 60**

The Tender Eight

Practice these things, immerse yourself in them,
so that all may see your progress.
(1 Timothy 4:15)

At first, prioritizing growth may not feel like you're accomplishing much; in fact, it may feel like giving up. Every moment you are convicted to be vulnerable or to listen intentionally and don't, the reality of growth becomes further and further from reality in your head. Again and again, you may fail to prioritize these things because it just feels useless, and then you'll feel beaten down and not enough.

Dear Eight, this is the challenge of being motivated by independence and wanting to grow in being vulnerable. You'll be constantly fighting the urge to not show weakness; you'll feel like vulnerability isn't worth the risk, and maybe you believe that even if you try, you can't change. These feelings are something Satan uses to make sure you never walk in the freedom of your worth in Christ.

Satan is all about stopping your growth from coming to fruition. I wouldn't be surprised if you even notice elements of spiritual attack as you prioritize growth. But that doesn't mean the growth isn't God's heart for you.

Going to Two in growth will feel painful at times, and you'll get discouraged. Remember that life is seasonal, and you will not achieve your ultimate state of growth here on earth. You cannot become your ideal self because you will never be without a sinful nature while you're still drawing a breath. However, this doesn't mean that you are not growing. By the power of the Holy Spirit, you are in the process of a beautiful becoming.

Don't let two steps forward and one step back discourage you. This is still moving forward; this is still growing.

Humility, vulnerability, and selflessness may feel utterly impossible at times, but you're trusting God for the outcome, not forcing it to happen yourself. You're trusting that trusting God is better than self-sufficiency or the illusion of control. You're trusting that God's Word is true, and that when He said that He would take care of you, *He will.* That growth is something He wants for you. Like the child at the edge of the swimming pool jumping into their father's arms, you're trusting that God is ready to catch you.

SHIFT IN FOCUS

Here, we are going to use 1 Timothy 4:15 as a guideline for action:

> *Practice these things, immerse yourself in them, so that all may see your progress*

"Practice these things"

Every new thing you've ever done required practice. Growing by going to Two is no different. Practice by listening intentionally, plan for things that fill you with compassion, and choose one vulnerable action that can be your next right thing. Every small step counts.

"Immerse yourself in them"

What verse that we mentioned over the last ten days really stuck out to you? I would encourage you to memorize it, write it out, and place it somewhere you will see it often. Immerse yourself in the truth of your worth in Christ, and you'll find yourself slowly but surely believing it to be true.

"So that all may see your progress"

Pick a couple of people in your life to share your big or small victories with. I hope you have a couple of people come to mind right away, but if they don't, there are plenty of Instagram or Facebook pages for Eights with followers who would love to cheer you on in your Eight-ish wins. Be bold and share them as something worth celebrating. Go get yourself a coffee, or have a bowl of ice cream! Life is hard, and any victories are worth celebrating with God and others.

BOOK RECOMMENDATIONS
FOR EIGHTS

Brené Brown, *The Gifts of Imperfection: Let Go of Who You Think You're Supposed to Be and Embrace Who You Are* (Center City, MN: Hazelden Publishing, 2010)

Jennie Allen, *Restless: Because You Were Made for More* (Nashville, TN: Thomas Nelson, 2013)

Bob Goff, *Everybody Always: Becoming Love in a World Full of Setbacks and Difficult People* (Nashville, TN: Nelson Books, 2018)

John Townsend, *Beyond Boundaries: Learning to Trust Again in Relationships* (Grand Rapids, MI: Zondervan, 2011)

Heather Holleman, *Guarded by Christ: Knowing the God Who Rescues and Keeps Us* (Chicago: Moody Publishers, 2016)

Henry Cloud, *The Power of the Other: The Startling Effect Other People Have on You, from the Boardroom to the Bedroom and Beyond—and What to Do About It* (New York: HarperCollins Publishers, 2016)

Peter Scazzero, *Emotionally Healthy Spirituality: It's Impossible to Be Spiritually Mature, While Remaining Emotionally Immature* (Grand Rapids, MI: Zondervan, 2014)

Shannan Martin, *The Ministry of Ordinary Places: Waking Up to God's Goodness Around You* (Nashville, TN: Nelson Books, 2018)

Jo Saxton, *Ready to Rise: Own Your Voice, Gather Your Community, Step into Your Influence* (Colorado Springs, CO: WaterBrook, 2020)

Alan Fadling, *An Unhurried Leader: The Lasting Fruit of Daily Influence* (Downers Grove, IL: IVP Books, 2017)

As the Enneagram has passed through many hands, and been taught by various wonderful people, I want to acknowledge that none of the concepts or ideas of the Enneagram have been created by me. I'd like to give thanks to the Enneagram teachers and pioneers who have gone before me, and whose work has influenced this devotional:

Suzanne Stabile

Ian Morgan Cron

Father Richard Rohr

Don Richard Riso

Russ Hudson

Beatrice Chestnut

Beth McCord

Ginger Lapid-Bogda

ABOUT THE AUTHOR

Elisabeth Bennett first discovered the Enneagram in the summer of 2017 and immediately realized how life-changing this tool could be. She set out to absorb all she could about this ancient personality typology, including a twelve-week Enneagram Certification course taught by Beth McCord, who has studied the Enneagram for more than twenty-five years.

Elisabeth quickly started her own Enneagram Instagram account (@Enneagram.Life), which has grown to more than 70,000 followers. Since becoming a certified Enneagram coach, Elisabeth has conducted more than three hundred one-on-one coaching sessions focused on helping her clients find their type and apply the Enneagram to their lives for personal and spiritual growth. She has also conducted staff/team building sessions for businesses and high school students.

Elisabeth has lived in beautiful Washington State her entire life and now has the joy of raising her own children there with her husband, Peter.

To contact Elisabeth, please visit:

www.elisabethbennettenneagram.com

www.instagram.com/enneagram.life